# Maintaining the DELICATE BALANCE in Christian Living

MW00488254

## Jay E. Adams

TIMELESS TEXTS
Woodruff, SC

Copyright 1998 by Jay E. Adams
ISBN: 1-889032-11-5

Printed in the United States of America

# Contents

# INTRODUCTION

For years I have wanted to write this book, but there has always been some reason to postpone doing so. Now, in retirement from the pastoral ministry, God willing, I want to fulfill that desire. I am glad I waited because, over the intervening years since I first conceived the idea, many new thoughts, angles and examples of what I wish to say have come to light. Others, held long ago, have matured. I trust that if this book successfully achieves its purposes, it will keep many from going astray in ways that distort and misrepresent the truth of God's Word. It is my goal to set forth a thesis that extends to everything that a Christian believes and everything that he does. If I am correct—and I believe that I am—the message of this book is important; indeed, it is crucial.

The history of the church could almost be written in terms of imbalance. (What I mean by this will become much clearer as you read.) There have been times when love dominated the church to the diminution of truth. At other times truth gathered such significance to itself that it all but obliterated love. Neither should have happened. Actually, as we shall see, neither actually happened, since truth cannot be truth (in any biblical sense) without the presence of love and love cannot be love apart from truth. But we shall examine that concept later in depth.

At the outset I wish to make a few preliminary points. First, when I speak of balance, I mean precisely that. I am not talking about synthesis, about compromise or about blending ideas, attitudes or actions into one. Nor am I speaking of Neoorthodox tension and paradox. All such notions are actually antithetical to balance. Take the Hegelian triad, for instance. Hegel set forth the Thesis-Antithesis-Synthesis model by which you might think and act. In attempting to move a person to your own point of view, you consider his present viewpoint as a thesis (A). Over against it you posit an antithesis (B). The melding of the two produces a synthesis (C) which in turn becomes a new thesis (D) over against which you place a new antithesis (E) which leads to a new synthesis (F), *ad infinitum*—or until you reach the place at which you wish to arrive. The method looks something like this (think of waltzing through history to the Hegelian tune):

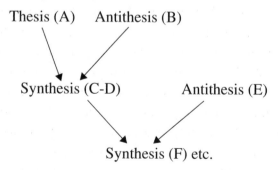

This method of thinking and acting, which still dominates much of Marxist philosophy and political action, actually amounts to the destruction of any and all balance. It is a method by which an idea, a viewpoint, an action is continually compromised until it no longer exists. Truth is altogether absent from the formulation. There is nothing Christian about this approach to thinking or living.

What then is biblical balance? What does it look like? The word "balance" itself tells you what you need to know. When a scale is balanced there is neither diminution of what is on one tray or on the other. The items on each are in exact weight and proportion to one another. To the extent that this is not the case, there is a lack of balance. If one side of the balance outweighs the other we say that the scale is unbalanced.

Life in a sinful world means there will be all sorts of forces impinging on you as a believer to destroy every balance you learn about in the Bible. The forces of dilution and compromise are as powerful as, indeed, those of addition, eclecticism and integration. Many times they do not come directly from Satan or the world that still "lies" in his power,[1] but from other Christians who think that you are too radical in maintaining a biblical balance in theology or in life. They too will call for compromise, for the watering down of biblical injunctions, concepts or ways of life in order to become respectable. They will present an antithesis over against one side or the other of the

---

1. See my book *Christian Living in the World*.

biblical balance (or against both) in an attempt to dim the white light of the truth and action that God wants to shine brilliantly in a dark world.

As we go along, you will notice that some of the items that must be held in delicate balance are theologically stated and others more practically set forth. Ultimately, the two cannot be separated. Theology determines life. Among other things in this book, you will consider such matters as the balance between predestination and responsibility, the balance between truth and love (mentioned above), the balance between optimism and pessimism, the balance between divine and human elements both in the writing of the Scriptures and in the process of sanctification. And you will see how maintaining balance, in an unbalanced world, is difficult but necessary.

It is my hope to observe the importance of proper balance in a number of specific areas, to point out some of the imbalances currently weakening the church, to describe the sorts of influences that tend to knock Christians off balance, and to suggest some of the ways in which to counter these. So far as I can tell, there has been a lack of interest in this subject that, consequently, has resulted in great confusion. It is my purpose, therefore, to help clarify what is happening in order to alert key Christians to the problem and to urge them to do all they can to rectify the situation in the church. The world will always lack balance, swinging from one fad to another. But there is no excuse for the church indulging in this arcing between ever-changing poles.

So, if you are ready, let's get started. We shall begin by trying to understand what this delicate balance is all about and why it is so important.

# Chapter One

# The Delicate Balance:
# Is it Scriptural?

The fire was spectacular. When our small barn was struck by lightning and burned to the ground, all we could do was watch. There was no hope of saving it. To the two black racers that inhabited that barn it must have been tragic!

But they coped. It was not long afterwards that we discovered them curled up in our bathroom near an electric heater. They had discovered our house, they had negotiated their way upstairs, and they had found the warmest place available to them. They were smart snakes! No wonder Jesus commands believers to be "wise as snakes but as harmless as doves" (Matthew 10:16).

You are to be like snakes. But not in all respects—in respect of their *wisdom*, Jesus says. According to Genesis 3:1, the snake was "subtle" (KJV), "crafty" (NASV) or "wily" (Berkeley). Outside of Proverbs, the same Hebrew word is used to describe sinful thought and behavior. However, as the usage in the Proverbs attests, there is a side to shrewdness (prudence) that is commendable. Obviously, it is that aspect of the concept to which Jesus alludes in this command. Christians are to be neither ignoramuses nor dullards. They are to be aware of what is going on and are to act prudently in view of that awareness.

But because of the many evil uses of craftiness and cunning, Jesus balances that command with the other: "Be as harmless as doves." There are some characteristics of doves that you would not want to imitate. Have you ever noticed the mess they leave under your bird feeder? You wouldn't want to be as annoying as they can be when they moan with mournful sounds hour after hour. But, while hummingbirds spend most of their time chasing one another from the source of sugar water, and even cardinals show their territorial nature by driving poachers away, you will never see a dove fighting. They just seem to await their turn, then swoop in to enjoy their feed.

Because Jesus wanted us to have a good sort of shrewdness, He was careful to distinguish that from the self-centered cleverness that cheats, deceives and plots against another. He *balanced* the idea with that of the harmlessness of doves. Plainly, the person who is *both* shrewd and harmless will live a balanced life in those respects, neither veering "to the right nor to the left" (Deuteronomy 5:32). This conventional phrase expresses the sort of balance in thought, attitude and life that is commended and commanded throughout the Bible.

Obviously, the concept of balance is biblical. But notice, this balance that Jesus carefully maintains by the two-fold command in Matthew 10:16 is not a matter of compromise, amalgamation, blending or tension. There is no paradox involved; there is nothing about the one (prudence) that is contradictory or antithetical to the other (harmlessness). But the two commands balance each other in such a way as to prevent the adoption of serpentine or dovelike ways that are inimical to the Christian life. One might end up as a confidence man were he to pursue shrewdness alone or become a Caspar Milquetoast if he were to seek in all respects to become dovelike. The emphasis on innocence helps one who is pursuing shrewdness to understand that all his "wisdom" in this regard is to be done for the benefit of others and the glory of God. Whatever he does must bless, not harm. He is to be as "simple, innocent or guileless" (*akeraios*) as doves. He is telling the disciples that as they go out like sheep among wolves (the Satanic forces that would oppose them), they are to strike this balance. They are always to use great wisdom and prudence in their ministries, but never to "put it over" on others by deceiving them, or "pull the wool over the eyes" of their opponents in what they do and say. Their approach must be entirely open, innocent, unmixed with guile or pretense. As Paul once put it, "This wasn't done in a corner" (Acts 26:26). As you can see, this is a delicate balance for them (and you) to maintain.

There are times when the superior, snakelike wisdom that a Christian possesses, because he knows the

Word of God, could be used to transgress that second command. And he may be tempted so to use it. But Jesus commands him not to use his wisdom that way. The welfare, even of those who oppose, must be uppermost in his thinking and in his actions toward them. On the other hand, there are times when in pursuing dovelikeness he might be tempted to roll over and let his enemies have a field day with him. In emulating the bird of peace he could go too far (if he didn't have the first command) and begin appeasing and compromising truth and righteousness for the sake of peace.

Obviously, then, from this very clear example of biblical balance we are able to see not only that such balance is an integral part of the Scriptural approach to living the Christian life and to Christian ministry, but also how important it is to understand and follow. Wouldn't you like to know a person who has these two qualities of snakelike wisdom and dovelike peace in perfect balance? He or she would be a fine person to have as a friend. Wouldn't you like to become such a person yourself? To do so, you must acquire and maintain biblical balance.

# Chapter Two

# Balanced Thinking is Essential

It is not only in the area of attitude and action that a biblical balance must be achieved and maintained. It is essential to be balanced in thought and doctrine as well. Take, for instance, the important issue of the inerrancy of the Bible. The liberals love to call the conservative view of inspiration a "dictation theory." They deride our use of the Bible as kissing the foot of "a paper Pope." They like to laugh at the poor Bible-believing Christian as a stupid, unscholarly obscurantist. But what they say not only misrepresents the facts, it is also slanderous of most conservative Christians.

We do not believe that most of the Bible was "dictated." There were portions of books that were given in such a direct fashion that they could be said to be dictated by God, but that is neither the only nor the primary way in which the Word of God was transmitted to us. According to Hebrews 1:1 it was "in a number of stages and in *a variety of ways* that God spoke to our fathers by the prophets." That doesn't sound like simple "dictation," does it? As a matter of fact, God spoke audibly (at Sinai, for instance); He spoke through dreams and visions (Genesis 31:24; 46:2), and He spoke by means of the Holy Spirit carrying along ("moving") the writers of the Scriptures (II Peter 1:21) as a wind catches the sail of a ship and bears it along.

In all of this there is a fine balance to be maintained. True, there are ignorant Christians who would maintain a strict dictation theory. This is what gives the liberals opportunity to tar all conservatives with that same brush. But their view is unbalanced. They seem not to understand that strict dictation is only one way in which God gave us His infallible Word— and indeed, the way in which He did so least frequently. What happened mainly was that God used the personalities, vocabularies, circumstances, etc., of the writers in such a way that what they wrote was precisely what they wanted to say, but at the same time exactly what He wished them to say. You can say that "Paul wrote" or that "God said" about the very same biblical word, sentence, paragraph or book. That is why in his second letter Peter could classify as "Scripture" along with other Scriptures, what he also said "*Paul* wrote" (II Peter 3:15, 16). Notice how naturally he does so.

Turn to Hebrews 10:15-17 and you will find that when the writer quotes the words of Jeremiah he introduces Jeremiah's words as the "testimony" of the "Holy Spirit" (cf. also Hebrews 1:5ff., 3:7-11). Clearly, there is a balance to be maintained here between the divine and the human (we shall see how that is true also in other areas as well).

The tendency of liberals is to exalt the human element in the writing of the Bible as the only or predominant one. By leaving out the work of the Holy Spirit, they come to the conclusion that since the Bible was written by sinful men, all the errors, foibles, inaccuracies, etc., that are common to sinful men must be present. They lack biblical balance in the matter. On the contrary, ultra-fundamentalist Christians, who may mean well, but think in a shallow, unbalanced way about their formulation of the doctrine of inspiration, emphasize the divine element to the detriment of the human. But when you recognize both, working together so as to preserve the individuality of the human writer and the integrity and inerrancy of divine revelation, you have a doctrine of Scripture that fits the facts. No one with any knowledge of Greek, for instance, can fail to recognize the differences in vocabulary and style between John and Luke. (That is why John's writings, which are so much easier to translate, are often used in first year Greek reading classes to encourage students.)

Balance, therefore, is vital to maintain in order to acquire and to sustain a biblically correct view of the Scriptures that is viable according to the observable facts. Neither the liberal nor the ultra-conservative is balanced in his view. Neither can properly understand or handle the Word of God as he should. Instead, each is bound to err drastically. On the one hand, the sneering liberal will look for errors; on the other hand the erring fundamentalist will treat all the biblical material alike, failing to understand that different writers use terms in different ways, with distinct meanings. Each distorts and destroys the facts about and the truth of the Bible.

Biblical balance maintains, with equal vigor, both the presence of human and divine elements in the writing of the Bible. It is a book that, because of the divine element, contains no errors, mistakes or misstatements. But it is also a book that bears the marks of each individual writer and the milieu in which he wrote (without error or diminution of truth). It is not difficult to understand that God, Who plans and controls all things sovereignly, could plan the situations, vocabularies, and styles of those He would use to pen His Word so as to produce under the inspiration of the Holy Spirit a book that in every respect could truly be called "His Word." But, because of the lack of biblical balance which I have addressed, many have not understood and, as a result, have themselves gone off into error and misunderstanding. Maintaining a *biblical* balance about these matters will protect you from any such imbalance on either side.

Notice that the biblical balance may be biblical in the sense that the truths it supports may be set forth explicitly by the Bible, or it may be biblical in the sense that when God does something in the Bible itself, He does it in a balanced manner. Balance may have several dimensions.

# Chapter Three

# Balanced Attitudes are Essential

It is not true that everything is so easily spelled out for us that we could never err. God gave us a Bible and expected us to study it. As Peter said about Paul's writings, "Some things in them are hard to understand" (II Peter 3:16). Much is simple; obviously the way of salvation is clearly, unmistakably, set forth. People are saved by what Jesus Christ did on the cross in dying for their sins. Christ's death and resurrection are declared to be the two points of the "good news" that were predicted in the Old Testament Scriptures and that one must believe for salvation (see I Corinthians 15:1-4). But everything is not that simple. While some things, as Peter said, are "hard to understand," others are not so "hard," but are not immediately apparent. It takes study to ferret them out. Then, there are other things that we learn by inference—by reasoning from one fact to another.

In this chapter, we now consider attitudes. An attitude is a fixed sentiment applied to things, events, and persons, based on past data that one accepts as accurate and at least somewhat universal. It is closely related to bias. It is important, therefore, to have a *biblical* bias or attitude. Again, we shall discover how important a biblical balance is in maintaining the right attitudes.

Are you an optimist or a pessimist? Your attitude toward people, events and life in general may be determined by which you happen to be. On what basis should one determine to embrace a pessimistic or an optimistic view of things? Once more, you should answer not on the basis of past experience or some other data; you must base your attitude on Scriptural data alone. Many think that the world, being filled with the effects of the curse and with the consequences of sin, is to be completely disowned. These pessimists go off on their own as monks or survivalists. They are wrong. Pessimistic asceticism, away from the world, is their *modus operandi*. Others, in a semi-Pollyanna fashion, see nothing but rosebuds. Christian Scientists are the supreme example of this equally erroneous tendency. Biblical balance, instead, leads one to adopt nothing but an optimistic/pessimistic attitude toward reality.

How can one be both a pessimist and an optimist at the same time? By maintaining a biblical balance about life. The Bible leads us to look on all that man does in his own wisdom and strength as "vanity." "All," we are assured in Ecclesiastes, "is vanity." The true Christian, therefore, is pessimistic about human schemes to clean up the environment, about man's ideas for improving society (he doesn't even have a standard by which to determine what is "better!") or about the latest political candidate and his policies.

He knows that neither experience nor the Bible lead him to put faith in man (Jeremiah 17:5). Because all are still sinners, the best of men lets his fellows down. Men are fallible, undependable, weak, self interested. How can a Christian be less than pessimistic about the best laid plans of mice or men?

Yet, I have said that the balanced Christian also is supremely optimistic. While on the one hand he is the most pessimistic of all men, on the other hand he is the most optimistic. Is this paradoxical? Are these two attitudes contradictory? Is there tension between them? Not at all. While the Christian is pessimistic about sinful men and all they think and do apart from the grace of God, he is optimistic about what God is doing and will do in this world for and in and through His church. Pessimistic about man; optimistic about God! That is the biblical balance. "We know that God is working all things together for good to those who love Him" (Romans 8:28). And we know that nothing goes astray. We bank on the words of Joseph, "You meant it to me for evil but God meant it to me for good, and to save a whole people alive" (Genesis 50:20). Nothing just happens; it happens just!

So, the Christian, with his double attitude—one toward man and all his works and another toward God and all of His works—thinks and lives with a philosophy in which disappointment though inevitable through sin, never surprises, never devastates him. He can handle suffering and pain, grief and loss since he approaches them in the proper attitudes. He expects little from man since any good he receives in this world of sin will be only temporary, and he is not shocked when he receives less. On the other hand, he is able to withstand the shock waves of trouble without despair since he knows that the final outcome is in God's hands—and it will be entirely good!

There is a large difference between this and grim Stoicism. The Stoic, in order to avoid disappointment, avoids both heights of joy and depths of concern. He tries to maintain a golden mean (*meson*) no matter what happens. He avoids all high excitement; his goal is "apathy" (the lack of passion). On the contrary, the Christian is passionate about what is wrong—he abhors evil and its effects. He never minimizes sin. And he exults in righteousness, joys exceedingly in the things of God and shouts and sings His praises. He is the opposite of the Stoic. He will allow himself to reach and experience the heights of every emotion that is biblically appropriate to every situation. He even "weeps with those who weep and rejoices with those who rejoice," thus extending his attitudes toward others in addition to himself.

The believer, following the Scriptures, agrees that sin "abounds," but he also recognizes that the grace of God is even more abounding (Romans 5:20). He is realistic; he does not cover his eyes or hide his head in the sand when appraising the doings of men—or of God! He need not find some middle ground in which today he is optimistic and tomorrow pessimistic, never knowing which attitude to adopt.

He does not waver. He firmly adopts both. And he does so without confusion, without contradiction or without stoic mediocrity. He is able to rejoice to the heights; he is able to plumb the depths. He is able to express the whole range of attitudes and emotions with which God endowed him. There is no need for restraint.

So, the delicate balance is important when you fall into trouble. Attitudes have a lot to do with emotions. How you approach a situation, what you bring to it, is crucial. As a balanced Christian, you may enter into affliction and experience all the sorrow and heartache that is appropriate, but you will never despair (cf. II Cor. 4:8, 16, 17). You may know the freedom of expression of the joy and praise that is found in the 150th Psalm, but you will not in your rejoicing overlook or excuse sin and misery. You must learn to enter into the command, "You who *love* the Lord, *hate* evil." Experience would never lead to this balanced position by which the Christian, superior to the Stoic in every way, can lead a life of victory and hope. Keep your balance in times of difficulty. Say with the Psalmist, "I was glad when I was afflicted so that I might learn Your law." And in it all, the reality of James' words comes home with force: "My brothers, count it an entirely happy situation when you fall into trials of various sorts" (James 1:2). That is something that only the balanced Christian may do!

# Chapter Four

# Balanced Actions
# are also Essential

I have already alluded to the fact that the entire Christian life is influenced for good or ill by balanced or unbalanced factors. What is true of thoughts and attitudes is true also of actions. When one acts in unbalanced ways, he thinks wrongly, and his attitude toward God, other persons and life is wrong too. All of these elements function together as a whole. You can't have one without the others. Thought leads to action; action influences further thought.

When John writes to Gaius (III John 1), speaking of him as one whom he "loves in the truth," he is speaking of two elements that, if not balanced, will mean that neither one is truly present. You can't have the one without the other. Church history has swung back and forth between ages in which Christians stressed truth to the detriment of love or, conversely, stressed love to the detriment of truth. But when you minimize truth, love becomes little more than a sticky sentimentality. It has no form or comeliness. It is amorphous mush! It is not biblical love. That is frequently what we see in many churches today where the "customer is always right" and where visitors set the agenda. They are served Christianity Lite, a religion which is but a pale reflection of the Christianity of the New Testament. Love is doing those things for others that conform to the truth of the Bible. The loving thing to do is to tell the truth even when it is unpleasant to do so. When biblical truth is eliminated, what is left may for the time seem comfortable, easy to live with and very relaxed. Because it retains a sort of sentimentality, the residue of biblical love, which is now little more than biblical mush because it lost its shape when the framework of truth was removed, may even be mistaken for love. Actually it does not endure long. It soon becomes dull, unsatisfying and—at length—hateful.

On the other hand, truth without love can become little more than sterile facts or, at worst, may initiate an inquisition. It must be enlivened by concern for those to whom the truth is taught and by a ministry of truth applied to genuine needs out of a concern that particularizes generalities into meeting individual needs and solving specific problems. The preacher who proudly spreads his net broadly, declaring himself to be only a preacher (or teacher), and fails to shepherd his flock personally, knows little or nothing about true ministry. He lacks the loving concern and care that implants truth so as to invigorate lives that, in turn, honor God and bless men. Truth can be cold, uninviting and even forbidding. The one imparting truth must always do so in the spirit of loving concern, whether he be a preacher or simple member of the church. Truth is eroded to the extent that it is divorced from the love that makes it come alive.

Love in this passage, as well as in many others, is love *shown.* It is love *in action.* In the Scriptures love begins with *giving.* When God loves, He *gives* His unique Son (John 3:16). That Son loved us and *gave* Himself for us (Galatians 2:20). And husbands who follow Him in loving their wives *give* themselves for those wives (Ephesians 5:25).

The letter in which John writes to Gaius is an indication of the fact that love is an active verb. Gaius had been thrown out of his church by Diotrephes for receiving the missionaries that John sent out. John writes Gaius to tell him that he had done the right thing in taking the missionaries into his home. John also informs Gaius that he will come soon to set things right and encourages him to keep up the good work until that time. John had previously written to the church to deal with the matter, but Diotrephes had the temerity to reject him and spread scandalous words about the aged apostle. The apostle of love would show love to Gaius and the befuddled church by coming to "remember" Diotrephes' evil deeds, presumably in disciplinary wrath. Once again, the delicate balance is achieved, in both past and contemplated actions.

Love in the truth is important. It is not a matter of Christians either loving or standing for the truth. There is no choice to be made. What could be more loving than to tell men the truth about their sin and their need of a Savior? What could be more truthful than to lovingly describe to a lost soul that sin and that need? Love and truth must be in balance; they ride best and do not wobble when they ride in tandem. Never forget that important fact.

There are people, however, who think it unloving to exercise church discipline, to expose the errors of those who lead the church astray and to counter falsehood with truth. The interesting thing is that when Jeremiah was faced with that sort of ministry, the need for the negative was so great that he was given two times as many negative commands as positive ones ("root up, break down, destroy, exterminate" as opposed to "rebuild, establish," Berkeley; Jeremiah 1:10). Sometimes, to balance out the situation that one faces, it is necessary to place the emphasis more strongly on one tray of the scale than on the other! If you are weighing feathers against lead that is supremely the case. The need to weigh demolition more heavily than construction seems to be the case in many (not all) church situations in our time. You cannot build on the rubble of the past. You must first destroy and clear in order to build. The ultimate goal, however, must never be a negative one (there are those who wrongly spend their time doing virtually nothing but demolition work) but a positive one (construction). You can't have the one without the other.

There are denominations today that do not grow mainly because of their insistence on truth to the near exclusion of love. This is a tragedy. The world *and* the church desperately need truth, but neither will hear when truth is presented in harsh, sharp tones that drive away rather than attract. Those churches that have tried to counter these tendencies by moving to the opposite extreme are equally as wrong. The answer, as in all that we have been saying in this book, is not an either/or, not an amalgam of, but an assertion of *both* love and truth *to the fullest extent of each*. What could be more attractive, more exhilarating, more helpful than that? All that I am saying here of denominations holds true also for local congregations and individuals within them. There must be love in the truth just as there must be truth in love. Pretense about either defeats both.

It is truth that brings about love. Apart from the commonalties of faith that believers hold to be true, there is no basis for Christian love. It is like a triangle with each individual at the lower angles and God at the apex. As each learns more about God and thus moves up nearer to Him, the persons involved grow closer together. Love for God growing out of a greater knowledge of God leads to greater love and knowledge of other Christians.

But it is also love that brings about truth. As persons learn to love God more, they want to know more about Him—just as a lover wants to learn more about the one to whom he is betrothed. As a person loves and learns, the learning leads to greater love which, in turn, leads to a desire to learn more, and so on. It is a cyclical process. Because love and truth are acted upon in relationship to the ones who are known and loved, they thus function in this manner toward one another. That is another reason why you must have both in balance. You will hardly spend time learning about that which you do not love. You will be able to generate precious little love for that about which you know little (or about which you have very uncertain knowledge).

Therefore, it is imperative to preserve the balance between love and truth. Whenever that balance is disturbed both love and truth suffer equally.

# Chapter Five

# Making Balanced Change

So far, we have seen the necessity of balance in thought, attitude and action, and have given examples of each. Now in the chapters that follow, I propose to simply take up a variety of specific instances in which balance is vital, in order to understand better how balance in these three general areas contributes to Christian living. I shall not make a point of identifying whether the material in any chapter falls under the area of thought, attitude or action, but shall consider each item in a more-or-less free manner.

Change is (or should be) very important to the Christian. From the outset of his Christian life he is strikingly aware of the fact that he is not the person that God wants him to be. Through justification he is reckoned (counted) to be perfect. The righteousness of Christ is applied to his account. But in actuality, he knows that he is far from having attained to anything like that record. Thus his concern (as Colossians 3 puts it) is to *become* in day-by-day living what he already *is* in the heavenly records.

The process of change in a Christian begins at regeneration and is called sanctification. In regeneration he is given spiritual life to believe the gospel and the capacity to live a life that conforms to the Scriptures. This capacity to love God and one's neighbor as God requires comes through the Holy Spirit Who is imparted to the believer at the time of spiritual conception (or "quickening;" cf. Romans 5:5).

The word sanctification means "the process of setting one apart more and more from sin to righteousness." It is a process that takes place over a period of time and is, therefore, progressive in nature. It is not a one-time act whereby one meets the requirements of some formula and is immediately catapulted onto cloud nine where from then on he leads a higher sort of life. No, it is that difficult day-by-day struggle with sin that the Spirit enables the believer to carry on successfully. Sanctification is growth. Where there is life, there is growth. Where there is spiritual life there is spiritual growth. Where there is spiritual growth and life it is because the Holy Spirit is producing it. This growth is elsewhere (Galatians 5) called "the fruit of the Spirit," which is described by some of its leading characteristics.

The balance of the human and the divine in the Christian life (discussed earlier) is obvious. In a number of passages *we* are commanded to produce those very qualities that in Galatians 5 are called the *Spirit's* fruit. (See my book *The Theology of Counseling* under the heading "The pursuit of fruit" for confirmation and discussion of this fact). Who, then, produces sanctification—the Spirit or the believer? Obviously, both. Once more we encounter the balance of the human and the divine: Christians produce fruit *by the Spirit.* That is to say, they do not do so in their own wisdom or strength. They receive wisdom and strength from the Spirit as He illumines His Word, the Bible, when they study it and apply its teachings to their lives. Sanctification is not an either/or but a both/and process.

Because of this double contribution to sanctification, it is necessary for the Christian to ask the Spirit to enable him to learn and to live what the Bible directs. Errors of all sorts occur when either one or the other of the two elements is ignored or minimized. It is wrong (though it sounds pious to say so) to declare, "I don't try to change my life. I allow the Spirit to do that! After all, if I do it, that is change brought about by a human being; not by God. So I just let go and let God." But if you turn to any book of the Bible, you will find commands having to do with your sanctification given to *you* to follow. Never once will you find the Holy Spirit commanded to do anything.

On the other hand, it would be wrong to think that a believer may make changes that are pleasing to God *without* the work of the Spirit in his life. Eliminating either the human element or the divine element in the process is a fatal error. Sanctification occurs whenever you obey the Bible through the power of the Spirit Who has been enlightening you to understand God's will as you have studied it. You (not the Spirit) obey, through the grace (help) imparted to you by the *Spirit.* That is one way in which balance plays an important role in the God-given change that occurs in the Christian.

There is also another aspect to change that has everything to do with balance. In Ephesians 4, Colossians 3, Romans 6 and 7, as well as elsewhere, we are instructed to "put off" the "old person" and "put on" the "new person." We are told to present the members of our bodies to Christ to produce righteousness by them just as we once presented them to sin in order to accomplish sinful deeds (Romans 6:19). In the process of sanctification, the Christian is to put off "fleshly" ways and put on "spiritual" ones. Without going into the various expositions of these matters that I have published elsewhere in depth (See *The Christian Counselor's Manual, The Theology of Counseling* and *Winning the War Within*) I shall simply affirm that Paul is saying that we must exchange old sinful habit patterns for new biblical ones. That is what the put off/put on dynamic is all about.

What am I talking about? I refer to the fact that not only must the old habits be put off, but that they must be *replaced* by new ones pleasing to the Lord. Too often Christians, like the world, speak of "breaking" habits. That is not the biblical way. Clean the house after a bad tenant has left and you will attract seven more of the same! You must replace him with a good tenant (see Matthew 12:43-45). The way the Scriptures set forth is not merely to "get rid" of a sinful habit but to replace it with its biblical alternative. Too frequently Christians fail to make progress in their lives because they concentrate only on breaking and getting rid of sinful habits. Without the biblical balance needed in this regard, they will continue to fail.

But it works the other way as well. It is not possible to successfully develop new ways while continuing in old ways that contradict and are antithetical to them. It is necessary to tear down before you can rebuild. There is no way of progressing in sanctification if a person refuses to repent of wrong patterns of living and is unwilling to replace them with biblical ones. Repentance must precede change for the good. Change, therefore, is a two-factored process. It does not occur by "adding" Jesus to your life so that things will go better for you. When Jesus comes into a person's life He shakes it up. Life can never be the same again. Jesus will not allow Himself to be "added" to the old sinful life unchanged.

So sanctification, in the final analysis, is simply what John the Baptist taught when he called Israel to repentance and then insisted on fruit that was worthy of repentance (Matthew 3:8). There was balance in his message. If "works," says James, do not follow faith, the latter is "dead" (James 2:26). He too insisted on a balanced change. Jesus also taught that when becoming His disciple, one must "take up his cross daily" (that is to say, put his own desires and ways to death) and deny himself (not deny himself *something*, but to deny his own *self*). This is the *put off*; it is one side of the balance necessary for biblical change. Then He went on to say, "and follow Me." That is the other side of the balance—the *put on*: following the ways Christ sets forth (Matthew 28:20). As in everything else in the Christian life, change is a two-factored process in which both factors must be present. To the extent that they are not, change will not occur. Change demands biblical balance.

# Chapter Six

# Judgment Must Be Balanced

"Judge not; remember that!" How often have you heard that retort when you have tried to warn against some heretical doctrine or when you have mentioned the need to talk to someone about his or her sin! What makes the statement so stinging is that the one who makes it is using the whip of Scripture to scourge you (cf. Matthew 7:1ff.). But on the other hand, what makes its use such an anomaly is that the lash is being used for the very purpose that Jesus forbids!

Consider Matthew 7 in the light of John 7:24: "Don't judge according to what appears on the surface; make a right judgment." Obviously, the juxtaposition of the two passages indicates that not all judging is forbidden, but that one must strike the right balance in this matter.

Clearly, Matthew 7 doesn't forbid making "right" or correct judgments. Indeed, properly understood, one can see that is precisely what it encourages. Jesus had healed a man on the Sabbath, thereby bringing the wrath of the legalists down on His head. He then explained that the judgment they had made about Him in this matter was all wrong. Reasoning from circumcision on the Sabbath, He went on to explain exactly why His action was proper. Their judgment was wrong. The judgment they made was built upon their man-made rules, not on the proper use of the Scriptures (vv. 21-23). So, in Matthew 7, judgment isn't forbidden—just the wrong kind of judgment.

Jesus warns people here about judging others when they, themselves, have the very same problems in their own lives but do nothing about them. He says they will be judged by the same standards they use to judge others (v. 2). And continuing, He calls such persons hypocrites if they don't *first* recognize and reckon with those sins (cf. His words about the log and the speck).

Note also two other things concerning Jesus' teaching in Matthew 7. First, after one removes the log from his own eye he is able to see clearly enough to remove the speck from another's eye (v. 5). It is not wrong to do so—if done as Jesus indicates. Second, the very first command from Jesus' mouth after His discussion of judging *requires* judgment of others. According to verse 6, you must determine who is a "dog" or "pig." Matthew 7 is a warning about wrong judging; it does not condemn all judging.

The unbalanced view of judging that many hold and the facile quoting of Matthew 7 in an improper manner have had the baneful effect of stifling the growth of discernment. Discernment (which, as the word indicates, is a "judging between" things and persons) is a very important element in Christian living. It is inculcated throughout the book of Proverbs, was sought by Solomon, given to him by God and commended to those who failed to attain to it (Hebrews 5:11-14). The writer to the Hebrews makes it clear that many had become "dull of hearing" because they were "inexperienced in the righteous Word." They were still craving milk instead of meat. Solid food, the diet of mature Christians, he says, is for "those whose perceptual faculties have been trained by practice to distinguish good from evil" (v. 14). That is discernment. That is judging (which means "dividing, separating")—of the right sort; judging by using the Scriptures as the Standard for judgment.[1]

It takes biblical balance to judge. The task is commanded in a hundred or so ways, so it is impossible to escape it. Every believer, in growing to maturity, learns how to judge rightly between good and evil. He learns how to distinguish genuine believers from dogs and hogs—at least in a functional way. Proverbs 18:13, 15 and 17 weigh heavily in all his judgments. He is careful not to believe a negative assessment of others apart from adequate testimony to back it up. He observes II Corinthians 13:1 and I Timothy 5:19 to the hilt. But he does judge.

One of the problems you will encounter in looking at the question of judging is the sin of judging motives. The heart, by which people make their decisions, is not accessible to you or me. It is God alone

---

1. See my book *A Call for Discernment.*

Who can weigh another's heart. We are told that "man looks on the outward appearance, but God looks on the heart" (I Samuel 16:7). That is a balance of tasks that we must learn and never lose sight of. In response to Jeremiah's question (Jeremiah 17:9) God is called the "Heart-Knower" (Acts 1:24; cf. also Jeremiah 17:10).

When one's actions are judged according to what another *thinks* are his motives, the judgment is not only unlawful but, more often than not, it is entirely wrong. You and I must operate only on the basis of a person's words and actions, what we see and hear. And then, only tentatively. We can never be absolutely sure of his motives, intentions, purposes or goals even when he tells us what they are. Thankfully, God left the realm of the heart to Himself; You and I should stay away from it! The difficulty of judging another person's motives ought to be apparent to anyone who has ever tried to judge his own. The heart can be deceptive—even self-deceptive. So we see that a balance is needed between obeying commands to judge rightly and not to judge wrongly—between judging another's actions and words and judging his heart's intentions. One of the evidences of immaturity is unbiblical, surface judgment.

There is a balance to be maintained between the human and the divine (what is God's part and what is ours in judging). This balance seems to come up in one way or another in everything we do as believers.

This is true because God is our Environment (Psalm 139). He is always there, always knowing, always active. He providentially participates in all that we do. His Spirit dwells within us and activates both our desires to serve and the service we render (Philippians 2:13). His Word directs us in all things necessary for life and godliness (II Peter 1:3, 4). Human thought and action, therefore, must always be related to divine thought and action (cf. Isaiah 55:8).

Judging is an unavoidable part of our lives (even those who rant against it do it). Therefore we must learn to judge God's way. That means acquiring and maintaining the delicate, biblical balance at all times.

# Chapter Seven

# Balance Your Two Worlds

Recently, an emphasis on Christians doing all they can to recover and reclaim this present world, upon living a life of wealth and health, upon getting involved in politics, legislation, bringing pressure upon others by strikes, protests, etc., has permeated the church. Others have strongly withstood any such emphasis, declaring that man's only concern here ought to be to prepare for the life to come. You live for two worlds; the heavenly and the earthly, the present and the future. How should you balance your concerns—how you spend your time and money, what you should do—as you consider both of these worlds?

The answer to the question above is not simple. It takes a good deal of biblical wisdom to give an accurate reply. While I cannot enter into all possibilities here, I hope I shall be able to sketch some parameters within which you should move and outside of which you will be throwing the good after the bad.

To open the discussion let's be clear that both the present physical world and the unseen world to come have been ordained by God and, therefore, have a place in His economy of things. Neither is to be despised. Neither is to be rejected out of preference for the other. Although the time in which we now live is called "this present evil age" (Galatians 1:4), that is no reason to become an ascetic who will neither taste, touch nor handle (Colossians 2:21). Such a retreat from the world is surely a non-christian reaction. Though monkish asceticism may appeal to some and commend itself as particularly pious and holy to others, the Bible speaks against it as "self-imposed worship and supposed humility" (Colossians 2:23). It is an unbalanced position. The Bible sets forth many obligations that the believer must meet in living the present life. He is not to coast while waiting for eternity. He is to engage in no eleventh hour thinking that impedes the progress he is to make in living for Christ in the here and now.

On the other hand, any neglect of the world to come out of an undo concern for this present age is equally taboo. The believer is not to build more and more barns, realizing that his soul (life) may be required of him at any time (Luke 12:21). He is to set his mind on things above and not on things on earth (Colossians 3:1). He is to maintain a light grasp on what he has amassed here in this life, to be willing to share, give or lose it if need be. He is to lay up treasures in heaven where nothing rusts or is eaten by moths. He is to weigh the relative worth of a world of sin in which there is suffering and sorrow over against the world to come in which only opposite conditions will obtain (Luke 12:21, II Corinthians 4:17, 18).

Clearly, this biblical balance is one that is tipped toward the life to come. Why is that? Because the present age is so deeply affected by sin and its consequences. But the Christian is not exempt from paying his taxes, from being a good citizen, from having an exemplary married life. How is it possible for these things to take place now? They may happen in this life precisely because he lives in relation to two worlds. The believer, while not physically present, has access to the powers of the world to come (Hebrews 6:4, 5). The God of the future is also the God of the present. By prayer he may enlist the help of the Creator of both worlds. He knows about the future life, lives in relationship to it (Hebrews 11:10, 14, 26) and may send treasures ahead against the day when he will live there. What he does now has eternal repercussions. He must never forget that when doing things here and now. So, while living in relation to two worlds, at every point—for his advantage or disadvantage—all he does in this world is bound up with the one toward which he is living and moving. The two cannot and must not be divorced. Life now is to be conditioned by the life to come. Proper balance will be achieved only when one realizes and reckons with this fact.

The Christian is to live zestfully in the present age. Though there is nothing here that will last, and those things that are not consumed with the using will be destroyed in the final conflagration (II Peter 3:11-13), he lives life to the full. Jesus came to give him "abundant life," and he must never forget that. The very same facts that may make cynics out of others are the motivating power for the Christian. A pessimistic outlook on a world that is perishing leads others to the thinking described in the cynical portions of Ecclesiastes. Unlike the Christian, they have no reason for living with verve. The Christian, on the other hand, finds all his hope and energy in thinking of and living for that which he knows will never perish. He sees the possibility of transforming things here into eternal treasures by doing so. With Paul he affirms that one's labor is not in vain in the Lord (I Corinthians 15:58). So he is "always abounding" in work here and now. The unbeliever knows nothing of this and so labors for this life alone.

What of the use of money and things? While holding them lightly, as I said, he does not hesitate to enjoy them, knowing that God has provided them "richly" for this purpose (I Timothy 6:17). On the other hand, when necessary, he can be content with only the bare essentials for life (I Timothy 6:6; Philippians 4:11-13). He gives to others in need (I Timothy 6:18), refuses to hope in uncertain riches, recognizes the trap and temptation money and things can be. He will never make the acquisition of wealth his purpose in life (vv. 9, 10). There is balance here.

The New Testament knows nothing of pressure exerted on the government by Christian pickets or protesters. In a day of great sin—including abortion and infanticide—the Christian church of the New

Testament is silent. Such worldly measures, indeed, were condemned by Jesus Who made it clear that His kingdom is not of this world, and that, therefore, His subjects would not fight to set things right. The weapons of their warfare would be persuasion; they would tear down the citadels of thought that unbelievers erect against a knowledge of God and take them captive for Christ (II Corinthians 10:3-6). In that way, righteousness would be spread to some measure throughout the world, although more would reject than would believe (Matthew 7:13, 14). The pressure that He exerts is a convicting, converting one. So, Christians should be active in preaching the gospel wherever they could. That is where they should expend their time, money and energy because it will reap eternal dividends. The hope of building or looking for a millennium here on earth is foreign to the Scriptures. That for which believers look is a "new heavens and a new earth in which righteousness is at home." But this follows the final wrap-up of all things (cf. II Peter 3:9-13).

This outlook is important for Christians. Heaven is their home; here they are pilgrims and strangers passing through. Yet, they are to be good travelers, spreading truth and wisdom wherever they roam (Acts 8:4). They are to care for God's present world—because how they deal with it now affects what they will be doing in the world to come. That is the proper biblical balance.

# Chapter Eight

# Balancing Predestination and Human Responsibility

All through the previous chapters we have spoken of the relation of the human and the divine. We have noted that everything the believer (the unbeliever too, for that matter) does he does in relation to God. Most of Psalm 139 deals with this matter. Whatever you do or say, wherever you go, God is there. He watches, He knows, He cares. The Psalmist is very clear about the fact.

That is providence: God is in control of His world and He is active in it. Your time and place of birth, your ethnic background, your family and everything else about you are items about which you had absolutely no say. Psalm 139:15 makes it clear also that like other people you were brought into existence and formed at God's behest. Everything about you demanded God's presence and work; that is a fact that you should recognize.

*Before* you were conceived, however, His influence was also dominant. God planned and brought about all things. That fact is called His predestination. That predestination is a biblical truth cannot be escaped by ignoring it. The very word occurs again and again. It means "to mark out beforehand." Take,

for instance, the words in Ephesians 1:4, 5. Paul tells
Christians that God "chose us in Him [Christ] before
the foundation of the world" and that "He predesti-
nated us for adoption as His own Sons." I will not
refer to the many other places where the same concept is plainly set forth but simply assume that if God
says something once that is enough. (Of course, you
might look up Romans 8 and 9 if you care to do some
in depth study of the question. You might also get a
copy of my book *The Grand Demonstration* in which
I discuss the subject at length.) Instead, I want to note
the relation of the human and the divine in predestination so as to help you acquire and maintain a biblical balance about the question.

People are always going off in one direction or
another—to one extreme or another—with regard to
predestination rather than looking carefully at what
the Bible says. Some say, "Well, if it's all predestined, what difference does it make whether I believe
or not; *que sera, sera,* what will be, will be." There
are even those who deny the need for evangelism
since all those predestined to eternal life will believe.

On the other hand, there are those who want to
avoid the issue altogether, who say that predestination is based upon God's knowledge of what man will
do in relation to Christ and that His predestination is
dependent on His foreknowledge.

Both positions are wrong biblically. Evangelism
is commanded throughout the New Testament and, in
Romans 9:11, Paul makes the point that God's pur-

pose is not dependent on what others do, but solely on His own choice. How, then, can we escape the idea that man is an automaton, simply playing a role in a great drama over which he has no control? The Bible consistently holds man responsible for his thoughts, attitudes, words and actions. How can that be if he is merely doing what was determined before the foundation of the world? Here we are concerned with the balance between God's predestination and man's responsibility for his behavior.

What is the answer to that question? To begin with, let us notice the fine balance with which Scripture brings predestination and responsibility together. Speaking of Jesus, Peter says, "This Man, delivered up by God's predetermined plan and foreknowledge, by the hands of lawless men, you killed by crucifixion!" (Acts 2:23). On the one hand, there is God's predestination; on the other, we see that those who crucified Christ are held responsible for the act—they are designated "lawless men." The verse holds God's predestination and man's responsibility tightly together as if it were the most natural thing to do (as indeed it is according to the Scriptures). There is no discussion of any difficulty in doing so. Peter simply thinks it is as ordinary as it could be.

But that is not all. In Acts 4:27 and 28 we hear Peter speaking again—this time in prayer. He says, "In this city it is true that Herod and Pontius Pilate together with the Gentiles and people of Israel gathered together against Your holy Servant Jesus, Whom

You anointed, to do those things that Your hand and Your plan had predestined to take place." There, once again, is the same sort of juxtaposition of human responsibility and divine foreordination. Not only was the event prophesied, predetermined (Peter is referring to a prophecy from Psalm 2, which he declares fulfilled by the death, resurrection and ascension of Jesus Christ), but he makes it clear that specific persons and acts were as well ("to do those things that Your hand and Your plan had predestined"). Yet these persons were held responsible for those acts (Peter called on them to repent).

How can we put these things together? First, notice that the very presence of prophecy fits the idea of sovereign predestination. What is prophesied had to be determined or it would be no prophecy. God is not a false prophet. Secondly, let's understand that the fact of predestination in no way lessens human responsibility. Whether you are able to understand or not, you ought to be able to see that the two are maintained in perfect balance in the Bible. But how can this balance be maintained? The answer is both simple and profound: God created persons who would *by means of responsible actions* bring about precisely what He had planned. That is to say, God's predestination was fulfilled not apart from, but by means of, choices and decisions that human beings would make for which they would be held responsible. God predestined *all things*. Not just the ends, but also the means. That is critical. In that sovereign plan, He determined to use responsible, human action as the means to achieve His ends.

Predestination is not fatalism. Fatalism says, "All is planned; it doesn't matter what I do." Predestination says, "All is planned; the plan will come to pass by means of what I do." Human, responsible action is absolutely essential to the biblical doctrine of predestination.

Again, it is a matter not of thinning out predestination or human responsibility. What must be done is to assert both with equal force and vigor. Let them stand side-by-side in your thinking as they do in the pages of the Bible. Keep them in perfect balance; abandon or weaken neither.

# Chapter Nine

# Balancing Love and Hate

Earlier in this book, I dealt with the balance that must be maintained between love and truth. But since love is so multifaceted, there are other balances that the Christian must maintain that involve love from a different perspective. Many Christians fail to consider the necessity to hate. Yet God is said to hate (Psalm 11:5; Proverbs 6:16) and Christians are commanded to do the same thing.

It is important for believers to understand that God has placed no emotion in man's makeup that has no proper use. Hatred, one of the stronger emotions with which man is endowed, of all the emotions is probably the most generally ignored. Beyond the readily-found (but wrong) wholesale condemnation of any hatred whatsoever, little is said about the matter.

In Psalm 97:10 we read, "You who love the Lord, hate evil." Doubtless this command strikes at the heart of a serious problem. Christians who recognize that they do not love the Lord as they should might consider that possibly the reason for their lack of love may be their lack of hatred for evil. In this sentence, there is a sturdy balance between the Lord and evil, between love and hatred. You might even say that one's love for God is dependent on his capacity for hatred toward evil. Indeed, one index for determining how much one loves God might even be how much ·he hates and abhors evil of every form.

Can you honestly say that you hate evil? Take a moment to ponder that question. To dislike evil is often as far as one's emotions extend. But do you actually *hate* evil? Do those things that are opposed to God's ways stir within you an antipathy so strong that you can accurately refer to that emotion only as hatred?

Unfortunately, for sinners, evil often has a strange fascination. It comes in many forms as Paul made clear when he wrote, "Abstain from every form of evil" (I Thessalonians 5:22). Truth is always one; evil is variegated. And the evil one knows how to wrap evil in enticing, inviting covers. Even Christians often like to play around the edges of evil of every sort. They, too, may become entranced with it. In Psalm 1 the course of decline is shown. First one "walks" toward evil, then he "stands," contemplating it and (if he fails to extricate himself) soon he is found "seated" in the seat of those who perpetuate it. This dynamic is seen in the life of Lot who, at first, merely pitched his tent "toward" Sodom. Next we find him living in Sodom. At the end he is listed among the elders sitting in the gate of Sodom. How can such a thing happen to one who is saved, as Lot was? It happens because the believer has not maintained the balance set forth in Psalm 97:10. "Can it happen to me?" you ask. Definitely. But it will never happen if you learn to *hate* evil.

But what is evil? The answer is plain: whatever God hates is what we should hate. Whatever is aligned against God or His work is evil. Whatever violates God's commands is evil. But what is the standard for knowing if something violates the commands of God and, thus, is evil? There is but one—and it is sufficient. It is the written Word of God, the Bible. In it one may find all the principles and practices that are necessary for discerning between good and evil (cf. Hebrews 5:11-14).

Some, who seem to think they can be more pious than the Psalms, speak and teach as if all hatred is wrong. That is an unbalanced and dangerous position to take, as we have seen. The true balance is never to hate anything God loves and never to love anything God hates. The hatred and love in Psalm 97 are not to be blended with one another any more than the good and evil that are mentioned. They must both be maintained with equal vigor. Taking a neutral attitude toward what goes on around one—particularly in Christ's church—is the antithesis to loving and hating those things according to biblical standards. It is altogether possible that if you have no violent hatred, you have little passionate love.

How does one begin to hate evil? Begin with Christ's church. And, when beginning with the church, start with the evil in the life of one member of that church—yourself! There is the proper place to begin to root out evil. As Jesus said, when He spoke of judging (q.v.), you must take the log out of your own eye before trying to extricate the speck from another's eye.

But it is wrong to end the survey of evil there. Whatever God hates to see in His church because it is disobedience and leads to a poor testimony before the world ought likewise to be hated by you. If you see a congregation in which wide open sin is tolerated without the application of church discipline, then it is time to have a strong enough hatred of the sin and its effects upon the witness of that church to the Lord Jesus as Savior that it will lead you to encourage the institution and application of church discipline. You cannot merely stand by if you are rightly motivated by strong hatred. This emotion is so powerful that it demands action.

Lastly, of course, you ought to have the kind of hatred of sin in the world that makes you avoid any and all entanglements with it. Your love for God ought to motivate you to testify to unsaved persons about the Lord—in no other way can you permanently put an end to evil. Laws, protests, reformatory movements, etc., are all temporary. What makes a permanent impact on society is the conversion of persons that make up that society. Hatred, then, should lead to evangelism.

But Psalm 97 speaks of loving the Lord. Just as passionately as you hate evil, you must love God. Love for God will motivate you to do all those things that promote His work and His honor. To glorify God is the way to love Him. It is the means for showing that love. Glorify Him by your own behavior and thought life. Glorify Him by your interests in His work and in His concerns; by aligning yourself in every way acceptable with those causes that stand for His truth and righteousness. But it is only as you hate the evil in yourself, in the church and in the world that you love God as you do those things that glorify Him in yourself, in the church and in the world. To develop and maintain a correct balance, you must love passionately—and hate passionately! Do you? Are you balanced in this regard? If not read this chapter again!

# Chapter Ten

# Balancing
# Resistance and Retreat

We are exhorted, "Resist the devil and he will flee from you" (James 4:7). But we are also told to "flee" various temptations and desires (I Timothy 6:11; II Timothy 2:22). How are these directives to be balanced? How is one to one know when to flee and when to resist? And, incidentally (but not of lesser importance) what does it mean to resist; to flee? How does a Christian fulfill those commands?

Here is a passel of questions for you, all of which are important to living a balanced Christian life to the honor of God. First, look at the background of these expressions: they have to do with warfare. In waging successful warfare a good general knows when to retreat and when to resist. Indeed, I Timothy 6, in which fleeing is enjoined, is followed in the next verse by the words, "Fight the gallant fight of faith." There seems to be little doubt then that Paul is speaking of two strategies to use in your war with the evil one.

Before looking at these strategies, it is important to emphasize once more that every Christian is in a war. This was declared by God Himself back in Genesis when He determined to put enmity between the woman and the serpent—and between their seeds (Genesis 3:15). You can no more avoid this war than you can crawl out of your skin. Just as when your country declares war, you are in God's war, whether you want to be or not. So, if war is unavoidable, it is important to understand and employ the very best tactics so as to win, and not lose, battles with the hosts of evil.

That God is concerned about such matters in this war with Satan is evident from the words of II Corinthians 2:11: "we aren't ignorant of his designs." It is knowledge of the enemy's plans, devices, methods, etc., that enables you to fight successfully for the Lord because this knowledge helps you decide when to "flee" and when to "resist."

Plainly, as the Bible indicates, the two most formidable weapons in the enemy's arsenal are murder and mixture. Throughout the years, he has successfully wielded both against the church. From the outset, as Cain murdered Abel his brother, the desire to wipe out those with faith has been evidenced. The entire Old Testament gives a clear indication of the way in which this method was used, and with what success. In the early church (along with those of our own time and the generations between) martyrs have gone to their deaths for the faith of Jesus Christ. They have resisted, and overcome (defeated) Satan, by the Lamb's blood (Revelation 12:11).

While in this country most Christians suffer little more than ostracism, persecution in its various milder

Sell your books at

forms still lingers. The success in the more forceful use of this tactic enabled the evil one to all but eliminate North African and French Christianity. But elsewhere, as Tertullian put it, instead, "the blood of the martyrs" became the "seed of the church." Satan has learned from this through the ages and has been far more successful in using non-lethal persecution of spiritually fat and flabby believers. It is in such situations that he must be resisted, as Christians learn neither to fear persecution nor the one who is behind it. If resisted, we are assured, *he* will flee.

The believer, however, is to flee temptations, both those that come from inner desires that are contrary to God's Word and those that come from without. While Jesus experienced only those from without, He taught us to flee from them by His own example in the wilderness as He repeatedly turned from evil suggestions to the Word of God. In each of the three temptations (cf. Matthew 4), because He turned from the temptation to biblical truth that countered it, He was able then to resist the Devil who at length fled, defeated.

The idea here, then, is not to longingly entertain thoughts of what it would be like to indulge a sinful desire or to yield to an evil temptation. You may not do this; to desire a woman in your heart, for example, is to commit adultery in the heart (Matthew 5:28). Flee from the temptation and turn to the strengthening Word which will free you from it and direct you in how to resist it. Then, having done so, you will be able to withstand those who oppose. Resistance requires all the armor of God—salvation, faith, etc.— that Paul describes in Ephesians 6. And both fight and flight must be done in the power of the Spirit. You can do neither, as God wants you to, by your own wisdom or might.

So, what we see in these two complementing commands—to flee; to resist—is that you must learn when to follow one and when to follow the other. As we have noted, often the ability to resist comes by fleeing the temptation. The principle seems to be that you must have God's Word in your heart that you may not sin against Him (Psalm 119:11). Clearly, then, when you do not know the right biblical way to counter temptation, it is the better part of wisdom to retreat for a time and learn. Then, armed with the Spirit's sword, you may sally forth into the fray. But you must not go unarmed (cf. Ephesians 6). Better to retreat today so that you may fight tomorrow than to attempt to fight today unprepared, thus leading to a defeat that may render your service at the front useless for some time to come.

Mixture, the second strong tactic of the enemy, has been more successful than murder. To blend error with truth, the world's philosophies with God's, the evil one's practices with biblical ones has weakened the church in every age. Satan hates God's Word. It is what binds men to God. It was His Word that he attacked in the Garden of Eden when he first questioned it, then distorted it and finally denied it. The "counsel of the ungodly" continues to do so today as it did then and in David's day (see Psalm 1). The only answer, again, is to refuse to become involved in eclecticism, in counseling, in adapting business principles to church growth or in any other area. The "pure" (unmixed) Word of God (I Peter 2:2) is what you must continue to depend upon rather than the contaminated views of those who would mix truth with error (Proverbs 3:5, 6).

Probably there are more Christians today in America than ever before, *per capita*, yet the church has never been so effete. Mixture is possibly the most successful tactic the enemy is using at the present time. Psychology is mixed with biblical principle, thus weakening the latter; people act out of pragmatic considerations rather than biblical commands—and go astray!

There is far too little willingness to study the Scriptures and far too great a desire to be accepted by unsaved persons around us. This is particularly true of Christian educators. They seem to have the idea that the more they resemble the world the more accepted they will be. But in doing so, they have failed to resist temptations from the world, the flesh and the devil. Rather, they succumb to these and, consequently, have little or nothing to offer poor sinners. They look so much like the world, they act so much like the world, that it is hard to tell them apart. (Again and again Peter had to note that Lot was a "justified" man since you'd probably never know it from the way he lived: II Peter 2:6ff.). Resist syncretism. Know and be on the alert for the wiles of the devil. He will attempt to get you to march to his tempo; you are to march to a different Drummer! So, you must learn to balance resistance with retreat. Learn to retreat so that you may resist! Otherwise, you will be in a continual retreat that is neither calculated nor desired. Better to know your weaknesses, deal with them, and *then* go out to battle.

# Chapter Eleven

# Maintaining Balance
# in Dealing with Fools

Proverbs 26:4 and 5 are not contradictory. Their close proximity is a studied thing. The author intended make the reader think about the balance that must be maintained between "answering" and "not answering" a fool. A fool, in Proverbs, is one who is foolish in his thinking, attitudes and behavior because he is foolish in his relationship to God. The word refers to those who have deliberately become obstinate or stubborn: to those who have resisted God's truth in favor of their own ideas. Therefore, the believer who wishes to please God will find himself from time to time (perhaps more often than he would care to have it so) up against a decision about how he is to respond to the foolish words or actions of some foolish person.

How does he do so? He is *not* to "answer a fool according to his folly" but, at the same time, *is* to do so. How do we square the seemingly contradictory commands? The solution is simple. One must never answer a fool *in the same manner* in which he acts or speaks. But he *is* to answer him according to the *content* of what he is doing or saying. If he disobeys the first command, then he becomes like the fool, adopting his ways. That is forbidden. But on the other hand, it is not right to stand by and allow the fool to get away with foolishness: he is to obey the second command lest the fool will think he has prevailed in his foolish thoughts, ideas or actions.

The balance is important. If a fool yells in order to emphasize his foolish thoughts, it is not right for the one responding to yell back at him. Keeping a cool, calm exterior, he is to refute the foolishness of the fool in a proper, biblical manner. He is not to become like the fool in this way. If a fool butts in on the conversations of others with his stupid comments, he is to respond in a tactful and non-obtrusive way. He is not to adopt the fool's tactics.

On the other hand, the fool must be shown that he is acting, speaking foolishly. He is to be brought to the place where his stupidity (and that is one of the notions of foolishness in Proverbs) is exposed as such. This may involve reprimands, conviction by means of biblical truth, reproof and the like. It may call for refutation of a logical sort from the Bible that others may see is correct but, alas, the fool may not. Nevertheless, foolishness is to be silenced, put down, so that it may not prevail. That is the idea behind not allowing the fool to become "wise in his own eyes" (he must be made to recognize his foolishness rather than think his actions appropriate because they were not effectively confronted).

There is, then, a ministry to fools. The only way they will ever escape from their foolish ways is if and when they come to realize their foolishness cannot be maintained over against truth and righteousness, and that they are foolish because they are acting contrary to the Scriptures. That is your task in relating to fools. But at the same time you must be careful not to adopt or imitate their ways. You must learn to be biblical both in the *what* and in the *how* of this relationship. The "according to" in these two verses refers to two different things. The first "according to" means "in like manner;" the second, "in response to what he has said [or done]." To give a proper answer, you must clearly distinguish between the two—as the second half of each command does.

Fools can be extremely aggravating at times. They also can be very destructive of good. It is hard to "put up with" them. But, following the commands of these verses, one may at the same time learn to follow Proverbs 15:1 and other verses that are appropriate to replying to a fool. It is difficult, but not impossible, to do so—so long as you stay close to the Bible in every aspect of your relationship to a fool. Who knows, now and then because of your balanced "answer," you may help a fool or two to repent and change.

# Chapter Twelve

# Balancing Faith and Works

James and Paul do not contradict one another. James stresses works as the evidence of true faith—and he is absolutely right in doing so (cf. especially James 2). Paul stresses faith as the prerequisite for living works (cf. especially Romans 4). He too is correct. They approach the subject from opposite directions, but they end up at the same place. The Bible teaches plainly that we are justified by faith without works. It teaches just as plainly that where there is justifying faith good works will follow. Without works, James says, so-called faith is *dead* (James 2:26). Hebrews speaks of *dead* works which are the result of unsaved persons trying to please God without saving faith (Hebrews 6:1).

The problem in the church has always been that some slip over the edge in one direction to the detriment of the other. Both must be maintained in balance as absolutely essential to true Christianity. The distinguishing factor is this: faith is the instrument by which the grace of God is received; works are the evidence that it has been. Faith brings about works (Ephesians 2:8-10). Works are the telltale evidence of salvation (Matthew 7:16, 20).

That last sentence is important. When some see passages that indicate men will be judged by their works, they often misunderstand. They mistakenly read "saved" for "judged." (Note Matthew 25:31-46 where the judgment is by works, but not salvation. Before judging, each already was either a sheep or a goat.) But that is a great error. A pie judging contest determines who is the best pie maker by the results (the taste, the crust, the filling, etc.) but those things have nothing to do with making the cook a good pie baker. That the baker is good is *determined* by the pie (the proof, we say, is in the pudding [here, pie!]—the product and its taste). But that is the same as salvation: the proof of salvation by grace through faith alone is in the works. One is *judged* to be saved by what that salvation produces. Works that please God are the product of a saved person. As Jesus once put it, if the tree is good it will produce good fruit (Luke 6:43-45). A bad tree produces bad fruit. You cannot turn this around.

So, the Christian is neither to become a legalist (thinking he can merit something from God because of his works) nor an antinomian ("It doesn't matter what I do or how I live so long as I have faith"). True faith is a grateful faith; a faith that wants to please God by bringing forth the fruit (works) of the Spirit. True faith declares that every good work that is produced *is* the fruit of the Spirit and allows its owner to claim no credit whatsoever. It recognizes that there is nothing in us to appeal to—that all is of grace.

It is utterly important, therefore, to keep these matters in careful balance, fully trusting in God's grace for salvation; fully obeying His Word because he has been saved. All ideas of merit must be removed; all ideas of laissez-faire Christianity must be rejected. One is to believe with all his might and is to pursue good works with unlimited vigor.

Have you gotten out of balance in either of these two directions? Few basic Christian concepts could be of greater importance. If you have any question whatsoever about the issue, you should inform your pastor immediately and get him to discuss and clarify the issue with you. Everything else in your Christian walk is dependent on having this fundamental, foundational matter clearly and definitely understood. Once again, balance here means neither rejecting nor thinning out either faith or works, but affirming both with equal force. Unbalanced thinking here will severely unsettle your life and your witness. It is imperative that you understand this simple but profound truth in order to live the balanced Christian life.

# Chapter Thirteen

# Balancing the Individual and the Community

Those who have stressed solidarity of the covenant community to the detriment of the individual have misunderstood the biblical balance in this matter. Likewise, those who have forgotten covenant responsibilities while stressing the individual alone have erred every bit as seriously. In our day, the pendulum of error seems to have swung to the latter rather than the former problem. In American "democracy," the emphasis is (supposed to be) on the individual. The Bible always maintains a perfect balance between the two from the beginning to the end.

In the garden, God dealt with both the individual and with the human race. Adam is set forth as the covenant head of humanity, acts representatively for us all and brings a universal curse upon our race. On the other hand, all that is said about him as such is said also about him as an individual. He personally was promised the blessings and warned of the curses as an individual as well as acting for us in a representative capacity. Adam's sin brought sweat to both his brow and yours!

After Joseph's experiences his comment to his brothers is revealing: "You meant it to me for evil, but God meant it to me for good and to save a whole people alive" (Genesis 50:20). There you have the two sides of this matter clearly set forth in harmonious balance. God acted in Joseph's life toward him as an individual, but also as one who was ordained to save the messianic covenant community from extinction. What God did had a dual purpose: one for the benefit of the individual, the other for the blessing of the community. That is the way that we see God acting throughout history as we read our Bibles. There is no either/or.

The people of Israel are truly a "people." What God does for Abraham's posterity, he does for the community *as a people* (Genesis 17). But in making the covenant with the community as such ("you and your seed after you") God likewise covenanted with each individual in that community. How do we know that for a fact? Clearly, when He says that He is concerned to see that each one circumcises his male child or *that individual will be cut off* ("he has broken My covenant," Genesis 17:14), God shows his interest in each individual within the covenant community. The one who refuses circumcision will be "cut off from the people." Here the interplay is between God and the community, God and the individual, and the individual and the community.

In Numbers 21 the fiery serpents are sent among the people because of their complaints about the trip to the Holy Land. The people, as a people, are judged. But each one who is bitten by a serpent may

be saved individually by looking to the serpent on the
pole that God ordered to be erected for the salvation
of individuals (and for the preservation of the people). In John 3, Jesus takes up the individual emphasis referring to the incident and uses it as an example
of looking to Him to be saved. But both work
together; the community and the individual must
never be divorced. How could it be otherwise? A people is made up of individuals.

In the New Testament, while the individual
emphasis may be more distinct, the new Israel, the
church is nevertheless dealt with as a whole. You
have a corporate entity addressed in each of the let-
ters to the seven churches in Revelation ("to the angel
from the church at. . ."). And things are said about
each church *as a whole*, as if the congregation in each
city had a solidarity that gave it a corporate personal-
ity. Jesus deals with it as a whole. (It is also true that
in a case or two He distinguishes some from others
within a congregation as being more or less faithful
than others.) But each letter ends up with a personal,
individual appeal ("to the one who. . ."). While one
belongs to the whole and is often treated as a part of
the whole, he is individualized to the extent that he is
thought of and related to by God *not only on a corporate basis but also on an individual one*. You are not
stuck with what happens to a body of which you are a
member. Remember, you, as an individual, have a
personal relationship with God as well. God is not
interested in large groups alone; He is great enough

to be concerned about the number of hairs on each one's head! The more individualized God's attention, the more we see His concern, His interest, His greatness.

Though Israel, as a nation, deserted God, Paul made clear there would always be a remnant who believed and did not desert. The nation that killed the prophets and finally God's Son would have its kingdom taken from it and given to a new nation that had not before been a nation—the church (Mark 12:9; Romans 9-11). Elijah whined that he alone was left to worship Yahweh but was told that there were 5,000 who had not bowed the knee to Baal. There was a nation, failing to read the signs of the times and thus unaware that the Messiah has come, but there was also Simeon who was "expecting the consolation of Israel" (Luke 2:25).

Today, you are responsible for all that goes on in your family, your congregational units, and in the church as a whole, and you will be dealt with as members of such. But you are also responsible for what you as an individual do in relation to God and to the community. You bear a double responsibility. You cannot divorce yourself from the community saying, "I am not responsible for what happens." On the contrary, you are responsible for your share of it, your impact on it, and will be held responsible. Nor can you say, "I am a member of a good, Bible-believing congregation; as such, I will simply bask in God's blessings on it." You, personally, have responsibilities before God that you, and you alone, can and must discharge. You are part of a body, but also individually members of it. That is the bottom line (cf. I Corinthians 12:27, especially).

# Chapter Fourteen

# Balancing Authority and Submission

The submission/authority problem exists not only in marriage, where sometimes very wrong emphases on authority or submission are made, but also in the three other authority/submission spheres of which the New Testament speaks. In addition to the *home* sphere, these others are: the *state*, the *church* and *business*. In Ephesians 5 and 6, Colossians 3 and Romans 13 (and elsewhere) you encounter the four biblical authority/submission spheres. Problems occur when any of these is ignored, when the authority of one sphere is confused with the authority of another or where extra-biblical spheres are imagined.

Sometimes, education is thought to be an authority/submission sphere, but there is absolutely no biblical basis for that notion. Ideally, all education should be attached to one of the four biblically-ordained spheres. The home should be responsible for basic education of children (see *Back to the Blackboard* for details), the state for the education of law enforcement and the armed services, business for specialized, professional training and the church for the training of ministers and elders. It is because those in education (and in other similar areas) have arrogated to themselves an authority that cannot be found in Scripture we are experiencing many of the difficulties that we face today. One Christian college near us has a black list of churches to which its students may not belong—or even attend! That is exactly backwards: the church ought to be evaluating schools—not the other way around. God established Christ's church; He did not establish an educational institution separate and apart from it. The church is a four-walled institution and stands alone on its own God-given authority. Educational institutions, on the contrary, are intended to be three-walled, attached by the fourth wall to one of the authority spheres.

But within the four legitimate authority/submission spheres there is sometimes difficulty as well. One problem is when one of these transgresses the bounds of the authority granted to it by God and trespasses on the territory of one of the other three. If, for instance, the state tells the church what it can and cannot do contrary to those rights, privileges and duties allocated to the church by God, there is trouble. To be specific, when the apostles were forbidden by the state to preach Christ they said, "We must obey God rather than men" (Acts 5:29). Not only did they acknowledge that the state had overreached its authority given by God, but that when it did so it no longer spoke with divinely-granted authority. It spoke only with the authority of "men." If the church requires the home to follow practices not biblical, it does the same. Balance is maintained between each of these four authority/submission spheres only when each remains within the area of its God-given authority. In other words, the authority of each is limited by biblical principles.

Let's take up the concept of a wife's submission to her husband. Ephesians 5 has much to say about the matter, as well as I Peter 3:1-6. But notice, the headship of the husband is not any old kind of headship. It is headship like that of Jesus Christ (not Hitler, Stalin or Saddam Hussein). As Ephesians 1:22 indicates He is "head over all things for the sake of the church." That is the sort of headship a husband is to exercise. The man qualified to be an elder is one who "manages" his own household well (I Timothy 3:4). The Greek word for manage (*proistemi*) makes it clear that he is to oversee the family and guide it, but is not to make all the decisions himself—just as any good manager today doesn't. He is to evaluate and use his resources well, as did the husband in Proverbs 31. So, a husband does not make unilateral decisions apart from taking others in the family into consultation. And what he does is "for the sake of" his wife.

She submits, as do the children, to her husband's authority (there cannot be two heads in a home). Someone must have that final authority. But she may not submit should her husband require her to lie, to steal, to commit adultery (as in a wife-swapping weekend), etc. All authority given by God in this sphere, as well as in the others, is solely within biblical parameters. God never gave anyone the authority to command anyone else to sin.

When the areas of authority are kept separated, when the persons act within the compass of biblical directives and when the spheres are limited to those ordained by God—and to those alone—then the proper balance is maintained. That this seldom happens in a world of sin is no excuse for any individual Christian himself not to follow these biblical directives.

As an example of someone operating two different ways in two of these spheres consider Romans 12 and 13. In chapter 12 the description of the private individual is given. He is to take no "vengeance." Vengeance belongs to God, he is told. But the same man lawfully acting as an agent of the state, to whom is assigned the duty of punishing wrongdoers, may be called upon to execute punishment as "an avenger of God." There is to be no vigilantism. There is no contradiction between the two chapters. Their juxtaposition, side by side, doubtless is intended to bring out the contrast between the individual's duty and that of the government official. Here, if anywhere, balance is clearly necessary. One must exercise his duties in each of the four spheres, when properly operating in that sphere, *to the full*. There must be no blending. Problems come when a person confuses which activities are assigned to two or more spheres. Balance clearly—wearing the right hat, at the right time, for the right purposes—is the key.

# Chapter Fifteen

# Balancing Tomorrow and Today

According to Matthew 6:34 the believer is not to concern himself with tomorrow; he has enough trouble to handle today. Here is the antidote to worry. Yet elsewhere (e.g., Titus 2:13) we are encouraged to place our hope on what God will do in days to come. How do we balance out these kinds of commands?

Plainly, one difference is that worry and anticipation of future blessing focus upon two distinct objects. The one who fears what tomorrow might bring and the one who looks forward to it, knowing that the promises of God will be fulfilled, are both thinking about the future, but in very different ways. The former is torn apart today (as the word "worry, anxiety" often means) by what he thinks might happen while the latter is strengthened today by his certain expectations. Another difference, you can see, is that the one who worries does not know what the future holds. The one who hopes has the promises of God upon which his hopes are fixed. Hope in the Bible is not equivalent to our modern day "hope-so" hope but is the anticipation or expectation of something that God has promised but has not yet brought about. Christian hope is in certainties.

The future, then, helps or hurts the believer depending on how he looks into it. When he uses the promises and prophecies of God as the reason for hope this can only bring joy and anticipation to him now. These truths, embedded in the pages of the Bible, give him something wonderful to look forward to. There is the coming of Jesus Christ, the righting of all wrongs, the eternal state in complete perfection of body and of soul. Such facts can only bring him pleasure within as he looks to the future. When he vainly tries to imagine what might happen tomorrow in a sinful world, however, it can only cause anxiety since there is no certainty in his own predictions. Indeed, in a world of sin, with a mind bent on the things of this world, he is apt to imagine all of the worst events possible. Rarely (though that isn't a rule) do these things occur as he imagines they might. Much of his worry focuses on feared outcomes that never happen. Even when his personal prognostications are on the mark, worry today does nothing to change the situation. Indeed, what changes is the individual himself who, because of excessive worry, may find it difficult to handle situations that do materialize.

Jesus' parable of the three men given money to trade until their lord returns is apropos. The first two traded and doubled their sum. They were praised by their lord. The third worried. He feared he might lose rather than gain. So he wrapped up the money and buried it. Then, at his lord's return, he presented it to him. His lord condemned him saying, "You wicked, lazy servant" (Matthew 25:26). Worry can lead to laziness. Because he can do nothing to control the outcome of events tomorrow, the worrying person does nothing about today. He becomes lazy rather than fruitful. The passage in Matthew 6:34 makes it clear that we are to assume today's responsibilities and not worry about tomorrow's.

Moreover, in that parable, Jesus describes the servant as having an attitude problem. He saw his master as hard, oppressive. He thought of him as one who picks up what he doesn't lay down, who reaps what he doesn't sow. Your attitude toward God and what you will encounter when you meet Him some day is all important here, now. You should look on your heavenly Father as One Who longs for His children to succeed. And, more than that, you should know that He does all things necessary to assure that you may do so. He provides His promises. He supplies directions in His Word. He gives the Spirit to enable you to interpret and to fulfill His requirements. He is anything but a hard taskmaster. Indeed, in the parable, the Lord's words are instructive. He says that it wouldn't have been wrong for the slave to put his money out for interest (that is, to invest it conservatively). The slave was wrong. His lord wasn't asking for something above and beyond his capacity. Nor is your Lord. He knows you and He expects you to live up to your capacities.

But even when you don't do all you might, He has provided for repentance, confession and fatherly forgiveness. God has made it possible for His children to retain a proper relationship to Him—even when they fail. There was no understanding of that in the slave's attitude. So, the future is important (knowledge of it is what helped Paul to continue in spite of hardships and suffering: cf. II Corinthians 3:12; 4:13-18). But how you anticipate it is every bit as important as to what sort of balance you maintain here and now.

The true balance is found when you joyfully submit your day-by-day plans to the Lord for His blue-penciling as James says you should. He is not opposed to planning for tomorrow (so far as one can legitimately lay plans) but, rather, to planning as if you were able to control the future, or as if you had any final right to say what should happen. You must always say, "If the Lord wills. . ." (in your heart, if not audibly; cf. James 4:15). In that way, life becomes an adventure, walking with God. That is the true balance to maintain. It is He alone who can keep your planning in proper balance and make tomorrow a blessing, today.

# Chapter Sixteen

# Balancing Covering and Counseling

Galatians 6:1 commands each believer to become involved whenever he comes across another Christian who is caught in sin from which he is not successfully extricating himself. He is to "restore" him in the "spirit of meekness." On the other hand, both Peter and James point out that "love covers a multitude of sins." In James 5:20 it seems that this quotation from Proverbs 10:12 says that "covering" means about the same thing that Galatians 6 does. To "bring back a sinner from the error of his way" is the means used to "cover a lot of sins." On the other hand, I Peter 4:8 seems to indicate that love covers sins by not making an issue of them. So does Proverbs (see the Berkeley version footnote on Proverbs 10:12), which contrasts hatred's "stirring up strife" by (apparently) identifying a matter with love's covering it so as to keep it down.

How do we balance these verses? Well, to begin with, it seems that the Proverbs verse is large enough to apply to both situations, as the two uses of it in the New Testament imply. That is important to understand in itself. Often, we are too ready to choose between things when there is every reason for including both.

If, for instance, a person seems to be entrapped by a sin—he is not extricating himself, as I said previously—he needs another Christian to assist him. The word "restore" is used of fishermen mending their nets and physicians mending a broken limb so as to make them function once again. It envisions a serious situation in which the believer is unable to function ("carry his own load") in the body any longer because of this sin. He, therefore, needs assistance: love shown by temporarily "bearing his burden" so that he may be brought back from the error of his ways to carry his own share of the load in the church once more. In other words, Galatians 6 and James 5 are speaking of someone who has ceased to function as a believer should.

On the other hand, the I Peter context is dealing with the general duties of one believer to another. It is similar to Colossians 3:13 where Paul exhorts us to "put up with one another." Doubtless, Peter is saying that we should not make an issue of every little rub. In love, we ought to learn to overlook such slights and inconsiderations by other Christians as may come our way. If, for instance, a husband and wife had to bring up every offense and deal with it directly, they probably wouldn't even be able to keep track of them all—let alone deal with them in some sort of family conference table or counseling session. No, what makes it possible for two sinners to get along under the same roof year after year is "putting up with one another" out of love. True love overlooks rubs and offenses, recognizing that the beam in one's own eye is every bit as large as that in another's!

There are people in the church who think that it is their task to tell everyone about everything over which they take offense. This is a very sad situation. As Proverbs warns, they "stir up strife" by doing so. It is when one is so "caught" in sin that he is unable to function as part of the body that another must counsel him. Believers must learn not to raise an issue about everything.

The time when difficulties between brothers and sisters must be brought up rather than covered is when, in spite of love, the problem throws the covers off. If a matter comes between two believers then they must deal with it. God will have no unreconciled conditions (cf. Matthew 5:23, 24). He wants matters cleared up quickly. But there is no excuse for a person to be so thin skinned that he cannot cover a lot of sins in love. Recognizing that we are all sinners helps. Recognizing that we must seek the honor of God's name more than the righting of all wrongs toward us is also important (I Corinthians 6:1-8; see especially. vv. 1, 7).

So you must learn to love more extensively. You must learn to do those things which make for peace in the church rather than stir up strife. Learn to cover a *lot* of sins—both by counseling and by overlooking those sins you can in love.

# Chapter Seventeen

# Balancing Theory and Practice

In academia perhaps the problem of imbalance between theory and practice is most prominent. One of the difficulties with our schools and, in particular, our theological seminaries, is that they are heavy on doctrine and theory and light on practice. But it isn't only in the schools that we find it difficult to keep these things in proper balance. On the other side, there are those who love to repeat, "No creed but Christ; no law but love." That statement is every bit as reprehensible as the idea of sending out ministerial students without the slightest understanding of what the ministry is like. It means that a person is willing to settle for a Christ he cannot know, a Christ without definition.

If there is to be no creed but Christ, there is no Christ! Or, rather, any man's idea of what he would like to make out Christ to be is the "Christ" for him—which amounts to the same thing. There *must* be truth, theory—*doctrine* if you will. Without the doctrine that grew out of the great Arian controversy and many others, we would have a hard time knowing what to believe about Jesus Christ. Without precisely formed doctrines garnered from the Bible, we cannot even talk intelligently. The *Westminster Confession of Faith*, for example, has an important role to play.

But, as Titus 1:1 puts it so plainly, truth is in the interest of godliness. Truth alone, without application, never leads to godly living. In His great commission Jesus spoke of "teaching to *observe*." It may seem pious to say "no creed but Christ, no law but love," but Jesus knew that the laws of love had to be spelled out definitively. We are not only to use teaching for life (to "observe"), but to see that Christians learn, and learn to observe (do), whatever Jesus "commanded" (cf. Matthew 28:20). That is specific; it refers to a body of instruction that Jesus left with us, now enshrined in the apostolic Word.

But doctrine, apart from life, is sterile. It has no outlet, no purpose, no meaning. All it can do is "puff one up" as he focuses upon his intellectual attainments (I Corinthians 8:1). Intellectual prowess is not a fitting goal for the Christian. As the body turns food into energy, so too he must learn to transform the truth into life. As a matter of fact, the *living* of truth, in itself, is not the end either. One must learn, live and then *minister* that truth to *others*. Otherwise all his learning is self-oriented, selfish. When ministry toward others and worship of God (loving God and neighbor) is the goal of truth and life then the whole picture begins to take shape. The proper biblical balance comes to the fore.

To assure greater balance, what may theological seminaries, for example, do? Here, a great deal might be said. I can but sketch out a few ideas. First, they can hire men who are pastorally oriented as well as scholarly. Too often the right man is turned down for one who has degrees—the penchant for acceptance in the academic world must be changed. Field work (as it is currently conceived) is not the answer. When men are placed out in the real world to observe and practice ministry under one who is already doing so full time, this procedure leads to bifurcation of the student body. One group says, "The preacher on the field is the one who has it," while the other group declares, "No, the teacher in the seminary is the one who really knows what's going on." The only answer to this is for the man who teaches a subject to go out with students on the field and demonstrate what he has been teaching. The integration of truth and practice in one and the same man is vital. Yet, how seldom does this happen!

Actually, the time is coming when many men will get their training in congregations, supplemented by courses they take through correspondence (by means of mail, video and other electronic media of the future). It is ridiculous for families to pull up roots, leave jobs and congregations and relocate in order to attend seminaries when there is enough material and good enough communication to do nearly everything from the home. Moreover, a student may select his own course of study from a wide variety of teachers in various places. In that day seminaries that do not become largely research and resource centers will dry up on the vine. At that time the practical may very possibly overbalance the doctrinal. Students will have to resist the temptation to allow this to happen.

Balance, you can see, may be upset or brought into being by a large number of factors, some of which seem quite external, but which may have a significant impact. We must never think that we can avoid dealing with the various factors in our milieu in order to maintain a biblical balance. Even computers can have a place in achieving a biblical balance! We must learn to use all of the gifts God grants us to bring the balance about.

The balance between mere reading, listening to taped lectures, etc., and interchange with teachers that comes through question asking, discussion and feedback about work done is another matter that may have to be faced at such a time. There may be a need for some travel (by students, teachers or both), some face-to-face interaction—or, at the very least, video telephone hookups. When some of us spoke about this fifteen years ago many laughed. Fifteen years from now we shall see who is laughing—at whom— about what!

So, the relationship of truth and its application to life and ministry is a balance that reaches into many areas. I have simply indicated one—the teaching of men for the ministry—but there are so many more. Can you think of five?

# Chapter Eighteen

# Balancing the Inner
# and the Outer

The heart is something that no human being can fathom (cf. comments on judgment); it belongs to God (I Samuel 16:7). Man can deal only with what another says and does. That is why judgment of another's "fruit" is the only way to make a functional judgment about him: "By their fruit will you know them" (cf. Matthew 12:33).

But what is this "heart?" Obviously, the Bible is not speaking about the physical organ within that pumps blood throughout the body. There is a spiritual "heart" of which the Old Testament and New Testament writers alike speak. Like the physical pump, the inner heart is vital to (spiritual) life.

"Heart" in the Bible does not mean what we mean when we use the word in Western society. We think of Valentine's day, of cherry cheeked cherubs, white and pink doilies and emotion. The biblical word refers to far more than feelings or emotion. You read of the "thoughts and intentions of the heart" in Hebrews 4:12, the heart acting as a conscience "condemning" in I John 3:21 and of the heart as the "hidden" inner person in I Peter 3:4. Consistently, the word stands for *all* that goes on inside you.

Often this inner aspect of a human being is contrasted with the outer person (cf. Matthew 15:8; Romans 10:9 where the "lips" and the "mouth" are contrasted with heart, as we see "outer appearance" is in I Samuel 16:7). Heart is the totality of what you are inside; with the Pharisees, the problem is one of imbalance: they wash the outside of the cup but inside is filth (Matthew 23:26). They are like whited sepulchers, clean outside and full of death within (v. 27). Jesus, like all the other scriptural writers who mention heart, then, understood it to mean the inner you. That is why in Proverbs we are told to "keep the heart with all diligence." Out of it flow "all the streams of life" (Proverbs 4:23). The heart, Jesus said, is like a treasury out of which comes good or bad—depending on what the heart is filled with (Matthew 12:35).

So the task of the Christian is to *keep* his heart. That is, to watch his inner life carefully. The heart is deceitful (Jeremiah 17:9). One must be very careful about what he observes within. He can even deceive himself. The heart may manufacture all sorts of excuses for sin. It may justify one before himself. The Christian needs a heart purified and regulated by the Word of God.

Within the compass of the word "heart" is what we call "soul." The soul is the nonmaterial part of man viewed *in connection with* the body. When God breathed into man the breath of life, he became a living soul. Soul is the animating aspect of man.

"Spirit" is the same entity viewed *as apart from* the body. Because He has no body, God is said to be a "Spirit." The Holy Spirit is never referred to as the Holy Soul for the same reason. In Matthew 10:28 we are commanded not to fear those who can only kill the body but cannot kill the soul. And in James 2:26 we are told that the body without the spirit is dead. Here, in both verses we see that the inner is contrasted with the outer.

No man but the Lord Jesus Christ Himself ever maintained an exact correspondence between the inner and the outer person. What you saw and heard when you encountered Him is precisely what He was within. The outer never conveyed a mistaken notion of the inner. So, too, ought your inner person and your outer person be in sync. That is the whole message about not becoming a Pharisee: one must not be a hypocrite. A hypocrite is one who says one thing but thinks another. He is one who represents himself as one kind of person by his behavior, but the fact is that he is decidedly different.

The balance between the inner and the outer does not mean that you must reveal all that is within you to everyone else. God alone knows your inner self. (Even you don't know it as well as He.) That is enough. What you are called upon to do is to accurately represent yourself to others. The phrase "putting the best foot forward" has a lot to do with this form of hypocrisy. A more biblical concept is found in the expression, "What you see is what you get."

"But," you say, "if I represent myself for what I am, no one would have anything more to do with me." In spite of what you are, *God* did not leave you. Instead, He sent His dear, only Son to die for you, Christian, so that you could have all the guilt of your polluted life removed as far as the East is from the West. Moreover, He put His Spirit within you in order to enable you to resist future temptation to sin and help you to live a life you need not be ashamed of. When the inner and outer are in sync with the Scriptures they will be in sync with one another. That is the balance for which to aim.

If the diversity between the inner and the outer you is so great that you fear to allow anyone to know you for what you are, that should indicate to you a need to make some rather large changes in your life! It is not wrong, however, to acknowledge sin and inner struggles with it (as Paul did in Romans 7), so long as it is also clear that you are regularly doing something about them (as Paul did in Romans 8). In one very practical sense, the Christian can say that his goal is to bring the inner and the outer into harmony with each other as they both harmonize with the Scriptures. That, in a nutshell, is the biblical balance to be achieved as one grows by grace.

# Chapter Nineteen

# Balancing Sorrow and Joy

In any number of places the Bible encourages joy and thanksgiving in times of affliction and sorrow (cf. James 1:2; Colossians 3:17; Philippians 4:4, 6). What does this mean? How can this be? If your little child is crippled by a drunken driver who runs his car up on the sidewalk and strikes her, are you to be happy about that? Are you to be thankful that it happened?

Here is a question that has perplexed many and, because of that perplexity, has led to strange and questionable answers. First of all, let it be known that God never encourages us to say, as some have, "Praise the Lord, anyway!" This insincere, glib statement made with a saccharine smile, is the antithesis of all that the Bible teaches about love and concern for others. When Jesus stood at the grave of Lazarus He did not say, "Thank God He died." Nor did He say, "Praise the Lord in spite of what has happened here." What did He do? He "groaned in anger within and was obviously disturbed" (John 11:33). Here His good friend had become the latest object of the curse of death and decay pronounced upon Adam's seed. Jesus responded with all the proper emotions. He was disturbed with sorrow; He was angry at what misery sin had brought into God's world.

No, it is not wrong for you to show your grief, your pain and sorrow, your anger, as all of these may be appropriate. To fail to do so is to fail to recognize tragedy and affliction for what it really is. Sin leads to misery. God explained that to Adam.

Well, then, was Jesus wrong in not giving thanks? Was He wrong in not counting the death of Lazarus "all joy"? Of course not. Jesus was never wrong about anything. And, let me point out—He *was* thankful and *was* joyful in the balanced sense that I am now about to discuss.

To be thankful for affliction and trial, to be joyful over sorrowful events, does not mean acting in some unnatural fashion. What it means is that knowing the promise of God to work out all things for the good of those who love him (Romans 8:28), the believer may thank God and rejoice over what God will ultimately bring out of the event. It is not during the trial itself that one rejoices with delight or gives thanks with great enthusiasm. Rather, it is in spite of the tragedy of sin that he gives thanks and finds joy in committing the whole matter into the Lord's hands. Through tears and pain he thanks. Through affliction and sorrow he has the deep seated joy of knowing it will all turn out for good.

Then, someday in the future—either in this world or the next—it will all come clear how God used the sorrowful event for good. Joseph was allowed this sort of knowledge in this world (Genesis 50:20), as was the apostle Paul (Philippians 1:12ff.). The Psalmist could say that he was glad to be afflicted since it helped him learn God's law (Psalm 119:71). But not all the ramifications of how sorrow leads to joy can be seen here and now (I Timothy 5:24); some only follow after one's death.

It is by faith in God's promises that we can rejoice in what He will do (cf. Hebrews 11; John 8:56). Faith is what enables one to keep his balance in time of sorrow, testing and trial. If you believe the promises of the Bible, you will not be inclined either to despair or to engage in some act of short-lived, ridiculous insincerity. Both extremes will be bypassed for a balanced approach to the difficulties of life in which, instead, you will fully experience the emotions appropriate to the sorrowful event and (at the same time) experience a joyful, thankful confidence that someday, some way, *how* this can be a "good" thing will become apparent. Faith keeps the Christian from imbalance. Don't let tragedy throw you off balance!

# Chapter Twenty

# Balancing General and Special Revelation

Psalm 19 deals with both general revelation and special revelation. So does Romans 1. In those two places we encounter most of the factors having to do with general revelation in particular. The interesting thing is that there are those who want to expand the area of general revelation far beyond what the Bible has to say about it. That throws everything out of balance.

All we can know from general revelation is that a Creator-God exists and that man bears a responsible relationship to Him. One can reason from the effects of the curse on creation (and is intended to do so) that God will judge for sin. More than that it is not possible to glean from general revelation. You cannot deduce the doctrine of the Trinity from general revelation. You cannot find the way of salvation by studying stars!

Special revelation picks up where general revelation ends. It further defines the God who may be known and the relationship sinners bear to Him, and to present the way of salvation from the penalty, the power and ultimately the presence of sin. It reveals to us all we could possibly need to know for salvation, for living the Christian life and for the balance that one needs to maintain between general and special revelation.

Revelation is *revelation*: the unveiling of truth by God. God takes the initiative. Man, apart from this revelation, would not know God's truth. Revelation must be distinguished from what has been called "common grace." God's existence may be known since He sends His rain on the just and the unjust, and gives breath to and sustains the life of those who hate Him all the days of their lives. But that is not revelation. General revelation has to do with God; there is nothing revealed about man's condemnation in hell or redemption from it.

What has so often been confused with general revelation is the idea that in common grace God *reveals* other truth. The slogan "All truth is God's truth" epitomizes it. Revelation being a God-initiated disclosure of truth to man is, however, something quite different from common grace. The two must not be confused. What truth (or half-truths) man discovers because God gives him opportunity, the smarts needed to do so and sustain him in doing it, is common grace. It is possible for sinful, cursed man to uncover facts about the creation even though affected by his sin so that he always puts a distorted twist on his discoveries. But, unlike *revelation*, man's *discoveries* are always man-initiated. In this they differ radically from revelation. Revelation is always true and inerrant, initiated by God; discoveries are not. About the one we can be certain enough to entrust our eternity to it; about the other we dare not do so.

Because of the confusion of common grace (in which God restrains sin and enables man to discover) and general revelation, we are told that God is revealing truth through such persons as Freud, Rogers, Maslow, etc. Nothing could be farther from the truth. Apart from the writers of the Scriptures, who were moved by the Spirit to write revelatory words, no man reveals anything from God to us. To rank the teachings of such pagans with Scriptural revelation is nearly blasphemous. Moreover, it is extremely dangerous. Whatever is placed side-by-side with the Bible becomes at first of equal authority with it, and in the end of greater importance. That is what happened to the "traditions of the elders" that Jesus claimed made the Scriptures "of no effect." The Rabbis had not intended to make their customs of equal or greater importance than the law of God. They only wanted to build a "hedge" around the Bible commands so that men would not be inclined to transgress them. But this pernicious idea—that God had not adequately hedged His word—became a curse to them. The same is true of those today who place the teachings of men on a par with the Bible: they have flooded the church with false ideas, unbelief and twisted notions of what the Bible does teach. As a result, in the minds of many, psychology is more powerful than God's Word!

Balance is achieved by not confusing things that differ and by assigning to the two types of revelation no more than the Bible does. Any imbalance here may lead to every other sort of error. Do you need to think more clearly about this matter?

# Chapter Twenty-One

# Balancing Law and Gospel

The way in which some contrast law and gospel, law and grace, you would think that you had to choose between them. The fact is that both are set forth in the Bible as from God. And it will not do to say that by law some were saved and by the gospel others were saved. The very idea that God ever saved anyone by the works of the law is inconsistent with all that the Scriptures set forth. There are not two distinct peoples, destined for distinct eternal locations, who will attain to them by distinct ways of salvation. That view is heretical. No man at any time has ever been or will ever be saved except by the blood of Jesus Christ. The very law itself recognized that "without the shedding of blood there is no forgiveness of sins" (Hebrews 9:22). And it is equally clear that it was not by the blood of bulls or goats that forgiveness was accomplished, but by the shedding of the blood of Jesus Christ alone (Hebrews 10:4).

The law was given, Paul makes clear, to drive men to Christ (Galatians 3:24). This it did by exposing the fact that, as sinners, they could not keep the law. Thus, they were forced to turn from their own hopeless efforts at self-righteousness to a Substitute Who died for their sins and Who alone kept the law.

That means that the purpose of the law was also gracious (Romans 7:9-12). The law, as Paul said, is "good." That it fails as a way of salvation is because we are not good. Righteousness comes not through the law, but through Jesus Christ.

The balance, then, is not to dispense with the law in favor of the gospel as some think we should. No. Rather we should use each rightly according to purpose for which it was given. Both must be maintained as firmly as possible. Without the law, men do not recognize their sin as they should. Without the gospel they are helpless, unable to find forgiveness and freedom from sin and its consequences.

To use the law unlawfully means to use it as a means of salvation, as the Jews attempted to do, thereby establishing their own righteousness—a righteousness which is totally unacceptable to God (Romans 10:3). Those who think that there is an earthly people of God who will be saved eternally by keeping the law are quite mistaken. That was the Jewish error against which Paul wrote again and again. No man, from Adam on, has been saved but by faith in Jesus Christ. The eleventh chapter of Hebrews is a sturdy witness to this fact. Jews who trusted in the sacrificial system for the forgiveness of their sins were wrong. That system was but a shadow of things to come. The blood of the sacrifices spilled on Jewish altars could *never* take away sins. They were not intended to do so. Those sacrifices were but shadows of the substance which was to come. That was their intended purpose from the beginning. They foreshadowed the coming Lamb of God Who would be slain on the cross. It was only those Jews who saw this in the sacrifices who were saved.

None of the material aspects of Old Testament worship was what God intended worship to be. Jesus made this clear in His conversation with the Samaritan woman (John 4:24). Circumcision was "nothing" in and of itself. It spoke of the inner circumcision of the heart which was the crucial element. All the rest of those types and shadows were similar. The Old Testament worthies who were saved saw what these types and shadows represented and trusted in the coming One Who was foreshadowed by them. The error of so many Jews (about which Jesus, John, Paul, Peter and the other New Testament writers spoke) was missing this significance. The error was to trust in the material (the outer), rather than in the spiritual (the inner) reality, of which the material was symbolic. The same is true today in the church of those who trust in ceremonies.

The gospel, then, was already there in the Old Testament. It was first preached to Adam (Genesis 3:15). Abraham believed it; Moses trusted in the coming Savior; David did too—and so on. The gospel is the "good news" that God has provided for us what we could not provide for ourselves. God sent His unique Son to live a righteous life, keeping the law, so that His righteousness could be reckoned to the account of all who believe the gospel. Those who believe find that their sins have been attributed to the Lord Jesus Himself. He was punished in their place, bearing the guilt and penalty for the broken law. Thus He provided both sacrifice and forgiveness as well as a perfect righteousness through law-keeping for them. This is the gospel great exchange. The sins of His people were cast on Jesus Christ Who bore them in their stead, and the righteous deeds of the Savior were written into their account.

So, in understanding the biblical balance between law and gospel, one who is truly biblical rejects the law as a means of salvation but establishes it as a means of exposing sin and demonstrating the need for a Savior. At the same time he declares that men are saved by grace through faith in Jesus Christ Who died for His elect people. There is no need to choose. There is no need to jettison the one or the other.

The same balance must be maintained in the Christian life. Trusting in one's own ability and wisdom, a believer fails to live up to the law which is his guide. He turns to the shed blood of Christ as the basis for continued forgiveness. Then he is able to keep the law to the extent that the Spirit enables him to do so. Sanctification is not by works but solely by grace. He does not begin the Christian life by grace and then live it by the law (cf. Galatians 3:2). The Christian always needs the law—to bring men to Christ and to reveal God's standard of righteousness.

# Chapter Twenty-Two

# Balancing Church and Family

I suppose there always have been those who think that they are putting God first by neglecting the family for the work of the church. There is a world-view in which God is allocated to one area of life to the exclusion of others. Those who adopt it fail to see that they may serve God every bit as faithfully by obeying Him in other areas. They do not realize that to do His will in regard to the family, work or any other activity as He commands is service as valuable as when driving a church bus to pick up children for church school. This false understanding of life is all out of balance. Pretty soon the one who adopts it finds his wife and his children or his boss forcing him to reconsider his views.

God is served whenever we obey His revealed will in any area of life. To serve God is to serve God! There is, however, a reasonable balance to be maintained between family, work, church and other areas of life that the Christian must think through in relationship to his situation in life.

Not everyone will find that the balance for him is the same as the balance for others. For instance, when Jesus spoke of time spent by those who remain single ("make themselves eunuchs") "for the sake of the empire from the heavens" (Matthew 19:12) it seems clear that he was saying the same thing that Paul was saying in I Corinthians 7:32-34. Those who are single may devote more time and energy to the direct work of the church than those who are not. But it is not wrong for those who are married to care about their spouses; that too is to honor Him who ordained marriage.

There are women, as well as men, who neglect their families for the work of the church. That is sin. They will spend long days (and nights) in busy work at church week after week. The congregation that allows such a thing to happen sins as well. There are times when I have said from the pulpit, "Now, we have this on Monday, that on Tuesday, something else on Wednesday, etc., etc., and the regular services on the Lord's Day. Please don't come to any of these services except those on Sunday unless you absolutely must. There is a need for all of them, but not all of you have the same needs. If you come to all these services, you will be sinning. We are not interested in numbers—simply in supplying that which is necessary to meet the various needs of all." That is quite a different approach from those who say, "Be sure to come out for the meetings this week—you must support your church!" Who is the church? It is the people. You support them by solidifying their families—not by tearing them apart with meetings!

The work of the church is important. In no way do I wish to minimize it. There is a time for meetings.

I am concerned only about balance. One should enthusiastically support church work, enthusiastically support his family, enthusiastically support his place of employment, etc. The idea is not to sacrifice one for the other. Often, when you hear Christians talking about "sacrificing," they are not so much speaking of the sacrifices *they* make as they are speaking about those they force other members of the family to make. I don't read anything in my Bible about causing others to make sacrifices. A minister, for instance, who "sacrifices" his family for the "work" is wrong. He has an unbiblical attitude toward his family. He is to be a husband to his wife as Christ is to the church; a father to his children as God is a Father to us. Does Christ "sacrifice" His church for the sake of His work? Does God do so with His children? There is no such concept taught in the Bible.

So, balancing the church—and all of its important activities—with the rest of life is a notion whose time has come. Many, during the heydays of fundamentalism, were taught the wrong thing about these matters. Now, within most of these churches, as well as among other conservative churches, these ideas have been challenged and much has been set straight at last. But the old ideas die hard. In many places they persist. There is something of a system of merit in the minds of those who will not let go of them. We should serve out of gratitude.

At the opposite pole, however, a kind of unbiblical rigidity can develop in which one refuses to do anything that might ever encroach on what he thinks is the proper amount of time to be spent in each area of his life. God's providence does not operate that way. There are times when we must bend the schedule. Jesus allowed His work to be interrupted by the needs that were presented to Him. The Gospel of Mark (among other things) is a study in how to handle interruptions and exigencies without getting off track or devoting too much time to distractions (for more on this see the *Christian Counselor's New Testament: Mark*). If you ever want to see perfect balance in the allocating of time and resources, look at how Jesus (as a single man) allocated His time. Flexibility, within basic limits, is what you see in His life. That is the answer—not rigidity.

In this day of home schooling there is also a tendency on the part of some families to become so ingrown that interest in others is neglected. When such a family is at church, it is always as a unit. When the family members are asked to do something for the Lord, they don't seem to be able to (or want to) join with others in doing it. They think that wherever they are, they must operate as a family unit. This sort of family isolationism is wrong. The family members need exposure to other Christians and must become involved in the "one anothering" activities spelled out everywhere on the pages of the New Testament. Just as an imbalance toward the church may hurt the family, so too an imbalance toward the family will hurt the church—and also the family in the long run. One family I knew raised children who were so strange in their attitudes that they failed to be able to get along with anyone else. They were entirely ingrown. This is a serious problem. Think of what it will be like when those children must leave home, establish their own families, become members of a church. Members of Christ's body should not become disjointed from the rest of the body so that they can no longer function in coordination with the other members.

# Chapter Twenty-Three

# Balancing Service and Authority

Two synonyms are *service* and *ministry*. All Christians are to be involved in the work of ministry (Ephesians 4:12). The task of the officers of the church is to help discover, develop and deploy those ministry gifts which each individual Christian has. But there is also a formal ministry; God has called some men out of His church to *office*. The primary office in the church is that of the elder (also called bishop or overseer). Elders "rule" and "manage" the church (see Acts 20; I Timothy 3, 5; Titus 1; I Peter 5:1ff.; I Thessalonians 5:12ff.) While their task is to "serve" (or minister) they also bear authority (they are to be "obeyed" and others are to "submit" to them: Hebrews 13:17). How is it that one balances authority with service or ministry?

It helps me to think of the manager of a motel. He is told by the owner, "Serve my guests." That is a large share of his tasks. If the towels are not freshly laundered or sufficient in number, he is to see to it that these problems are remedied. If something is wrong with the toilet, he is to care for that as well. Whatever he can do to make his guests happy by meeting their needs he is to do. By serving his guests, he serves his employer.

The elder of Christ's church has a similar task. He is to serve God by serving the members of the flock allotted to him by the Chief Shepherd of the church. He is to meet their needs, help them in times of trial and difficulty, see to it that they are properly fed on the Word of God. But in the Bible God also calls on him to discipline them whenever it is needed. These two tasks we call "the care and discipline" of the church. The two must always be maintained in balance. Imbalance in either direction can lead to the destruction of the body.

How does he know when to exercise either one or the other? Consider the motel manager once more. If the guests say, "You have such a fine rug on the floor; would you send someone to help me roll it up and put it in my car? I want to take it with me" or "May I borrow a screwdriver to remove this lamp from the table; it would look perfect in my own home," the manager draws a line at such *service*! Indeed, he now must exercise *discipline*. Service has its limits. He says, "You take those things and I will call the police!" He serves his guests, yes—but only so far. When they transgress the parameters set up by the owner of the motel, his service to his owner is not to "serve his guests" but to prosecute them!

Service in the church does not mean enabling its members to sin! One ministers to the flock only in the ways that the Master has set forth in His Word— ways that will bless them and build them up in their faith. There are limits to ministry that may not be transgressed. If and when they are, the Owner of the church is no longer being served. Elders must exercise church discipline (for details, see my *Handbook of Church Discipline*).

In one sense, church discipline *is* service. When a believer does that which is wrong it usually harms himself, his loved ones, his church and the Name of his Lord. If he continues doing so, he must be confronted for the good of all those mentioned. Church discipline is a privilege. It is designed to bring a straying sheep to repentance. According to Matthew 18:15ff., depending on how soon he repents, he is to be confronted by a growing number of persons in order to restore him. This is a privilege that is not to be withheld from a Christian who needs it. The elder asserts authority as one means of ministry whenever that means is called for.

It is wrong, however, for an elder to strut around through the congregation like a cop with his hat cocked on one side twirling his nightstick and tapping people on the head with it in order to let them know that he has authority. That is a misuse of the Lord's authority (cf. I Peter 5:3). But on the other hand, when he is required to assert it ("You may not continue in that adulterous relationship any longer") he must do so without fear or hesitancy. To show love, he asserts the authority that God Himself provided for that purpose. In thus asserting this authority, he must always do so with the good of the offender in view. The honor of God is what he wants to bring about by the reclamation of the sinning believer.

The elder must understand that service and discipline are two sides of one door. Balance means sacrificing neither one for the sake of the other. You can't have the one without the other. Indeed, the only thing that ultimately draws the line between the church and the world is church discipline. Where it is absent, it is hard to know whether you are dealing with a true church of Christ or not. On the other hand, where ministry in meeting need is absent, again one must wonder whether there is a church or only a prison where elders are little more than wardens or correctional officers. The balanced church is one in which the elders exercise care and discipline over the members. The two go together. Are they balanced in your church? If not, what needs to be done?

# Chapter Twenty-Four

# Conclusion

I hope you have gleaned from the reading of this book—that Christianity is not some limiting religion in which one has always to choose between alternatives. Those who represent it in this way are quite mistaken. The fact of the matter is that the Christian faith, like the Bible upon which it is based, is not narrow, but "exceedingly broad" (Psalm 119:96). If you have noticed anything, it ought to be that Christianity maintains both sides of what many have wrongly thought to be opposing alternatives. We don't choose to love or hate; as Christians we are obligated to do both—properly, under the right conditions. We are not obligated to choose between the individual or the community, the family or the church. We are to serve God by heartily throwing ourselves into the service of and love for both. On and on—in areas not mentioned in this book—the same point must be made. Christianity is not a small, cramping faith that forces its adherents to make tragic choices; it is sweeping in what it encompasses. It views all the world as God's world and points out the proper way to relate (with enthusiasm) to every aspect of it. It is a religion not of compromises, in which its beliefs and activities pale into vagaries and dullness. It is bright and exciting in all that it demands.

I hope also you have developed an appreciation for the possibilities of moving boldly into areas that, otherwise, you might have feared even to encounter. Fear of leaving undone what ought to have been done while tackling something new should not cause you to hesitate to do other good things. The lesser duties do not exclude the greater; nor do the greater exclude the lesser (Matthew 23:23). Neither in the service of the church are you required to neglect yourself or your family in the service of God. Indeed, it is to serve God that you serve. Yet you are never to become so self or family oriented that you neglect the church. You should serve God by enthusiastically doing good for both.

There is an either/or quality to our faith, it is true. When the biblical antitheses are set forth you clearly see it. There is truth and error, light and darkness, good and evil, faith and doubt, clean and unclean, righteousness and sin, the broad way and the narrow path, those who are within and those who are without, the counsel of the ungodly and the counsel of God, etc. These are choices between the things of Satan and the things of God—and they are sharply set forth so as to create an antithetical mode of thought in relation to all such issues. But this mindset may not be carried over into choosing between the things of God. Here, there is abundance. At times, there may be seeming alternatives, but both are to be entered into rather than to be chosen between. That is the message of this book.

Finally, there is one other message. Because so much is to be included in Christian living, because the range of good things that God has for us to do and to enjoy is so wide, it is possible to fall into various imbalances. It is possible to emphasize one good thing to the exclusion of another. Because one wishes to include all, he may blend things into muddy grays and browns rather than maintaining their pristine primary colors. The Bible knows nothing of weary compromises. The delicate balance to be maintained is the balance that enables one to live an exciting, productive, joyous Christian life. Whenever some imbalance is present, to the extent to which that imbalance exists, the productivity and the joy of one's life is impaired. The excitement wanes. So the challenge is always to understand, pray for and continue to attain to all that the Bible sets forth—in as perfect a balance as possible! May God bless you as you endeavor by His grace to do so.